HITLER, MY NEIGHBOR

ALSO BY EDGAR FEUCHTWANGER

*From Weimar to Hitler: Germany, 1918–33*

*Disraeli*

*Imperial Germany 1850–1918*

*Bismarck*

# HITLER, MY NEIGHBOR

## MEMORIES OF A JEWISH CHILDHOOD, 1929–1939

Edgar Feuchtwanger
*with* Bertil Scali

Translated from the French
*by* Adriana Hunter

*Other Press*
*New York*

Originally published in French as *Hitler, mon voisin: Souvenirs d'un enfant juif* by Éditions Michel Lafon, Neuilly-sur-Seine Cedex, in 2013.

Production editor: Yvonne E. Cárdenas
Text designer: Julie Fry
This book was set in Sabon with Kabel by Alpha Design & Composition of Pittsfield, NH

10 9 8 7 6 5 4 3 2 1

Library of Congress Cataloging-in-Publication Data

Names: Feuchtwanger, E. J., author. | Scali, Bertil, 1969- co-author.
Title: Hitler, my neighbor : memories of a Jewish childhood, 1929–1939 /
    Edgar Feuchtwanger with Bertil Scali ; translated by Adriana Hunter.
Other titles: Hitler, mon voisin. English
Description: New York : Other Press, 2017. | "Originally published in French
    as Hitler, mon voisin : souvenirs d'un enfant juif, by Editions Michel Lafon,
    Neuilly-sur-Seine Cedex, in 2013"—Title page verso.
Identifiers: LCCN 2017004211 (print) | LCCN 2017015223 (ebook) |
    ISBN 9781590518656 (e-book) | ISBN 9781590518649 (hardcover :
    alkaline paper)
Subjects: LCSH: Feuchtwanger, E. J.—Childhood and youth. | Hitler, Adolf,
    1889-1945. | Hitler, Adolf, 1889-1945—Homes and haunts—Germany—
    Munich. | Jewish children—Germany—Munich—Biography. | Munich
    (Germany)—Biography. | Jews—Persecutions—Germany—History—20th
    century. | Holocaust, Jewish (1939-1945)—Personal narratives. | BISAC:
    BIOGRAPHY & AUTOBIOGRAPHY / Personal Memoirs. | BIOGRAPHY
    & AUTOBIOGRAPHY / Historical. | HISTORY / Jewish.
Classification: LCC DS134.42.F48 (ebook) | LCC DS134.42.F48 A313 2017
    (print) | DDC 940.53/18092 [B]—dc23
LC record available at https://lccn.loc.gov/2017004211

*Today I am firmly convinced that basically and on the whole all creative ideas appear in our youth.*

—ADOLF HITLER, *MEIN KAMPF*

*Today it seems to me providential that Fate should have chosen Braunau on the Inn as my birthplace. For this little town lies on the boundary between two German states which we of the younger generation at least have made it our life work to reunite by every means at our disposal.*

— ADOLF HITLER, FIRST LINE OF *MEIN KAMPF*

I like it when she plays this piece for me. A piano minuet. She told me Mozart wrote it when he was my age. I'm five. I listen to the notes, it's very pretty. I'm on the floor, swimming on the parquet as if it were a lake. The armchairs are boats, the sofa an island and the table a castle. If Mama sees me she'll scold me and say I'll dirty my suit. I don't care. Anyway, it's itchy. Now I'm lying flat on the floor under the chair. I have my gun so I have nothing to fear if the French attack. I'll stay hidden.

I was scared again this morning when the poor came and rang the doorbell downstairs where the caretaker lives. Mama went down and I watched from the top of the stairs. They had beards, and holes in their clothes. They wanted money. They were selling shoelaces. Mama came back up and walked right past me, not even noticing me. She found a loaf of that bread I love, the white bread with a golden crust woven over the top of it like a girl's braids, and she took it downstairs. When she handed it to the poor people they smiled at her and went back out into the street.

They came again this afternoon. She was still playing the piano, the piece that gets really fast at the end, she was laughing and I was spinning on the spot, watching the room swirl around me.

The beggars were back. I was first to hear them hammering at the door. Mama stopped playing and went down to open it. One of them was really yelling. He said their house had been taken, and their savings, and they'd been thrown onto the street with their children. He said it was because of the Jews. I was scared, I wanted to cry. Mama was kind to them and one of the men said he knew her, a tall, fat man with a big white beard.

"She's a Feuchtwanger!" he boomed.

He got hold of the nasty little guy who was yelling and pulled him away. He explained that he'd been at school with Uncle Lion and had even read his books. I hid upstairs, keeping watch with my rifle. I wished I was invisible, like in the book they read to me at bedtime. The man with the beard winked and told the little guy he was a pain with his nonsense about Jews. Mama thanked him sweetly and asked Rosie to fetch some sausages. Rosie's my nanny. I rolled away like a soldier and she didn't see me when she walked past. Her white apron and black dress made a rustling sound. I was under the chair. I watched her go to the kitchen. She muttered to herself in dialect, the different language she uses when no one's listening. She said the poor were idiots; she cursed, saying we didn't have all that many sausages, and she didn't know what we'd have for dinner tonight. She came back with the sausages and gave the fat man a smile. He thanked her, blessed my mother and headed off with the gang.

Aunt Bobbie, our upstairs neighbor, came down and talked to Mama. I couldn't really hear. I think Aunt Bobbie told her my uncle would make trouble for us if he wasn't careful with his books. Uncle Lion's a writer. He makes up stories for grown-ups. Mama smiled at Aunt Bobbie and promised to let Uncle Lion know. She tried to reassure her, telling her not to worry, saying the beggars were just poor people who'd been in the war and had lost everything. I ran to the window to watch them. They were ringing the bell at the building opposite, gathering together a little group with others from up the street.

I've been watching the poor through the window since this morning. They're still there outside our building. What if they attacked? I have my rifle! When Mama spotted me earlier, she smiled, came over to me, drew the curtains and said it was time for tea. I asked her what a Jew was, and she whispered in my ear that I was too young to understand.

I may be five but I follow everything. I know what a Jew is! One time Papa talked to Mama about them in front of me. She asked him to change the subject because I wasn't old enough, but he said I wouldn't understand and kept talking. I played with my little cars on the floor, pretending not to listen. But I heard everything. They were talking about the Nazis, who don't like the Jews. The Jews means us, the Feuchtwanger family. I've known that for ages. I already talked about that with Rosie. We're all the same, Rosie told me when I asked her, only the Jews don't believe in the baby Jesus. But I know he was real. Rosie told me all about him. He had long hair and was very kind. Bad men hung him on a cross, put nails through his hands and feet and killed him. I wanted to know if the Jews were the villains. Rosie said they weren't, the Nazis were mixing everything up. It was the Romans who killed Jesus, and anyway, he was a Jew himself. It's a very old story, from another age, another time, long before I was born, or my parents, or their parents, or all their ancestors, before the days of cars and cities; it happened in an ancient country that no longer exists, over the mountains, the fields, the rivers and the sea. She opened the neck of her blouse and showed me a tiny golden cross on her chest. She said I could hold it. I touched it softly, she brought it to her mouth and gave it a little kiss, then she kissed my forehead and said I was her little darling, and that all children and all people were made of one flesh, that we were all children of the Lord, and Jesus said we should all love each other. She looked kind of sad, and I snuggled close to her.

So when my parents were talking about the Nazis I knew what they meant. I wanted to tell them that the

Nazis were getting the Jews mixed up with the Romans. But I decided to keep pretending I was playing on the floor so I could hear what else they had to say. We were in the study, the room where Papa keeps all his books in shelves that go right up to the ceiling. He has thousands of them. He's read them all, and likes looking at them, picking one up, opening it, closing it again, fingering it.

■ ■ ■

My parents are sitting on the green velvet sofa. I like it when they're both here. Sometimes he touches her face. He gazes at her and she looks at him admiringly. She tells him he's handsome and she loves him, but his mustache tickles when he kisses her! He says that her kisses make his glasses steam up. My father is handsome and elegant. I'd like to wear clothes like his, a white shirt and a tie instead of this itchy woolen suit, and a nice jacket with wide stripes like his. He always tells me I'm too young.

Shafts of sunlight warm my legs, which stick out from my hiding place. I listen to their conversation. They're talking about Uncle Lion and Adolf Hitler. Uncle Lion thinks Hitler will be leader one day and when he is he'll kill all the Jews. I don't know who Hitler is but my lips wobble and I want to cry. I come out of hiding and sneak into my parents' arms. They don't understand why I'm sobbing. Neither do I.

■ ■ ■

I'm riding my elephant on wheels. His name's Hannibal, like the emperor who fought the Romans with elephants. He attacked the Romans by crossing the mountains in winter. When I sit on Hannibal my feet don't touch the ground. On his back, I'm big and tall. The window is open; the sounds of birds and cars come in from outside. I take Hannibal over and lean on the windowsill to look out. It's a beautiful day. Cars have their roofs down and I can see the passengers. There's Aunt Bobbie, who lives upstairs. She's with her sweetheart, Duke Luitpold of Bavaria. A duke is like a prince or a king, and Bavaria is the other name for our country: my parents say we live in Germany, but Aunt Bobbie, the duke and Rosie insist we live in Bavaria. Mama and Papa say they're German, Aunt Bobbie and the duke that they're Bavarian.

The duke's car is driven by a chauffeur. I can see his white gloves and his hat with gold braid and a shiny black peak to protect him from the sun and the wind. The car is like a carriage, lined with beige leather. The duke really does seem like a king. He's wearing a top hat, a tailcoat that makes him look like a penguin, and just one eyeglass. It's a monocle. I call him "the Magician" because he manages to balance that piece of round glass in front of his eye. Aunt Bobbie is wearing a big white hat; her rings flash in the sunlight. She sees me and waves. "Bürschi!" she cries. That's what I'm called at home, it means "little boy" in Bavarian. I wave back to her. The duke says hello too, waggling the golden handle on his long regal walking stick. Aunt Bobbie shows me a little parcel tied with red ribbon. I know it's a box of candied fruit because she gives them to me all the time. I can't wait for her to get up here and give them to me, I want it to happen right now.

A big black car draws up on the other side of the street, and they turn to look at it. A chauffeur in military uniform walks around the car and opens the passenger door. A man steps out, looks at Aunt Bobbie, then the duke, then up at me.

He has a little black mustache, just like Papa's.

Rosie makes me jump slamming the window shut. She draws the curtains, undresses me and puts me to bed for my nap. I hate nap time. I don't like the bars on my bed either.

Eyes closed, I can feel Rosie's gentle hand on my cheek. I fall asleep.

I dream that the man opposite turns into an ogre, he catches us and wants to eat us. He has big bushy hair and long pointed fingernails, like Struwwelpeter, the horrible boy in the book on my nightstand. With his hooked nails and bristly hedgehog hair, the ogre chases my family through the streets. My parents hold my hands but they run too quickly for me. I slip and fall behind, my mother comes back for me, the monster's catching up. Wicked Friedrich—the little boy who whips his maid, kills cats with stones, pulls the wings off flies and throttles turtledoves—is in my dream too, throwing chairs like cannonballs.

I don't know whether I like the book *Struwwelpeter*. It shows Jesus giving presents to well-behaved children who eat up their soup, play with their toys and meekly hold their mother's hand. He has angel's wings and a crown. He looks like a little girl in a nightgown, kneeling in the snow. A star shines over his head. A bayonet and a military drum hover on the page among the presents. The book tells the terrible stories of naughty children. Friedrich beats his dog cruelly. Little Pauline perishes in the flames that burn her ribbons, her hair, her feet and her eyelids till all that's left of her is a small heap of ashes and her little polished shoes. Her two kittens cry and their tears make a pool of water. Children jeer at a boy who's black from head to foot, and they're punished by Nicolas, who dips them in ink. They end up flat as a sheet of paper, like shadows. A man with huge scissors cuts off Conrad's thumbs to stop him sucking them, and that story terrifies me because I suck my thumb. Meanwhile Gaspar dies because he never eats his soup, and Robert disappears into the sky, carried away by his umbrella. It's all jumbled up in my mind. They float through the air, fly around me, become misshapen, elongated, then disappear...

I'm hot. The back of my neck's wet.

It's a bad dream.

I'm standing up in bed.

I step over the bars, climb onto the small rattan chair and look out of the window.

The street is quiet. A curtain moves in the building opposite.

■ ■ ■

Rosie and I walk to the park every day. On the way we pass Herr Hitler's house. Rosie always walks slightly faster then, and stops listening to what I'm saying.

Yesterday my hat fell off outside his building and she didn't hear when I told her. We had to go back. A guard had it in his hand. He was tall, dressed like a soldier, and he said I was very cute, that I'd be a good brave German when I grew up. Rosie didn't want to stay a minute longer, she dragged me away, walking quickly, clutching my hand too tightly. She looked annoyed; I didn't dare speak. She almost shouted when she reminded me that I mustn't talk to strangers.

■ ■ ■

Mama is always at home, whereas Papa comes back late, after my dinner. But Mama wasn't here this afternoon. She came home with Papa, just after my nap. They were carrying parcels and laughing. They told me I was their little treasure and wouldn't stop kissing me.

Today's a big day, a special day, because Uncle Lion is coming to dinner. My uncle who writes books, the ones the beggars and the lady upstairs talk about.

My father gave a loud cheer when he saw the table, and he threw his arms in the air, thanking Rosie. Mama also said she'd done a good job and I definitely think I saw her blush. Rosie pointed out that she and I had set the table together, and the excess color started to fade from her pretty face. My parents clapped, and this time I think I was the one blushing…This morning Rosie had ironed the big tablecloth, the one she keeps in the laundry room. It's also my room: when anyone talks about me or my toys, they call it "Bürschi's room," and when there's linen to iron, fold or put away, they say "the laundry room." We share it during the day.

Rosie had placed the handsome candelabra in the middle of the table; it has lots of branches and once belonged to my grandmother, my father's mother, who died when I was little. My parents sometimes show me photos of her and tell me she adored me, and I vaguely remember a lady with a walking stick. Rosie told me that, if my parents didn't mind, I'd be allowed to light the candles. When I saw how pleased they were with the beautifully set table, I asked whether I could.

"Why not," said Papa. "You'll do it no worse than a real rabbi." And I don't know why but everyone laughed. I blushed again, of course.

The steam from the bath makes condensation on the windows and I can draw on it. Rosie doesn't like me drawing on the glass, grumbling that she'll have to clean it later, but my pictures vanish when we open the window. The bathwater's scalding, it took me some time to get in. First my toes, then my ankles and calves. I waited awhile till I was used to it. Then I could sit down. Now it's stopped burning. I'm quite happy here with my toys; I sing and play wars, the Germans against the French. My uncle Berthold was wounded in the trenches. He told me the Germans were unfairly said to have been defeated when they'd actually won more victories. Papa wasn't pleased when he heard Uncle Berthold telling me about the war. He scolded him and I felt like crying. Uncle Berthold has a beard, and I think bearded men always look sad. But I don't want my uncle to be unhappy. To cheer him up I make him win in my bath-time war.

But he's not the uncle who's coming to dinner this evening. That's Lion, the uncle who writes books, the ones the beggars and the lady upstairs talk about.

Mama tells me I don't remember him because he doesn't come to our house much. I'm dying to see him, I can't wait!

Papa joins us in my laundry-room-bedroom. He has a skullcap on his head, a small fabric hat. He has two of them in his bedroom, his and his father's, the grandfather I never met. He doesn't wear them but I know they mean a lot to him because I'm not allowed to play with them. My mother tells him he looks ridiculous. He says it will amuse Lion and, with a wink, he puts the other skullcap on me.

Mama draws the muslin across the window. It's a magic curtain that lets the light in but hides us from the outside world. So the neighbors can't look in. And she leaves the room.

Rosie calls me and I go to have my dinner in the kitchen, which is full of delicious smells as usual. She's cooked me my favorite sausages, white ones, well done. She slips them onto my plate from the pan, and I can hear them spit. She pours over the juices and adds golden potatoes.

I didn't hear the doorbell but Uncle Lion has arrived. He and Papa are standing over me talking. Their voices are almost identical. They look alike, like twins. Lion is shorter and wears big, round clown's glasses. Aunt Marta, his wife, is here too. I haven't met her before. She's beautiful; she has a hat perched on her hair, which she wears lifted up off the back of her neck; her lips are red, her teeth white and her eyes brown. She winks at me and I look away.

Uncle Lion says in a joking voice that I have just the right headwear for eating sausages. I don't understand. Papa looks embarrassed. He explains that I'm wearing the skullcap in Uncle Lion's honor and because it's the Sabbath, like when they were children. Uncle Lion laughs out loud and says those were crazy days back when they were children, and at least I didn't have to have *payot*. Now they both laugh and I don't know what they're talking about. Uncle Lion explains that *payot* are ringlets of hair in front of the ears. In the old days all Jewish men wore their hair like that. They dressed in black and wore kaftans, big cloaks that stood up to all weathers, the wind, the snow and the rain. When they were little, my father and my aunts and uncles—there were seven of them in all—respected these traditions.

"Luckily, all that's over for your father and me," says Uncle Lion.


I'm under the table. I can see Uncle Lion's shoes, they're black and white, like the fur on the panda that Rosie showed me in a book. They smell of polish. My father's shoes are very shiny, the windows are reflected in them, small and distorted. My mother's wearing her pretty high-heeled shoes that make her legs longer. Aunt Marta's legs are crossed against each other, like two people hugging. Through the fine black mesh of her stockings, it looks as if her skin is dusted with beauty spots. I listen to their conversation from my hiding place. I can hear the words, and repeat them to myself but don't understand them. I try to remember them and dream up a meaning for them. It's like being lulled by music, mysterious incomprehensible music.

"My dear Marta bought herself a new car this week," says Uncle Lion.

"It's a BMW," Aunt Marta trills in a voice as high as the top notes on the piano. "A coffee-colored sports car. I think there are only two or three women in all Munich who can drive, one being your neighbor's sister, Friedl. Everyone watches when I drive past in the street."

"But it's madness!" says my mother, and it's my father who retorts:

"Come, come, my darling," my father says. "It's certainly less of a burden than a horse and carriage. No need for a stable, or straw and hay. And still less a coachman!"

"It's very practical," Aunt Marta agrees. "We're going to the country this Sunday. Would you like to come? Would you like to bring the boy? He's such an angel."

"Oh, if you'd seen Hitler's face when we parked!" says Uncle Lion. "He arrived at his place at the same time as we reached yours. He didn't recognize us."

"Thank goodness for that, my darling, with what you said about him in the paper," Aunt Marta says.

"So what? We're still a republic, aren't we?" That was my uncle's voice, and then Mama joins in:

"They're saying his book, *Mein Kampf*, is the best seller in Germany."

"No, mine is, *Jud Süß*."

"You should be careful," says my father. "Everyone at the office keeps talking about your next book. *Success*, is that right?"

Uncle Lion sniggers, "It's true that your Duncker and Humblot tend to publish Herr Hitler's friends…"

I don't understand everything they say. But I like listening. I copy their words, like a parrot.

"I've heard," Uncle Lion continues, "that your protégé, Carl Schmitt, wasn't completely averse to the woolly theories of those bastards the SA.* Don't tell me my little brother's publishing company is tending toward the far right like all the rest?"

"Not at all," my father retorts with a strange laugh. "I can assure you Schmitt isn't a racist. Besides, we publish other authors. You should read the Englishman Keynes, for example, even if his *Economic Consequences of the Peace* might be bedtime reading for our eminent but offensive neighbor. I'm very proud to be his publisher."

"I was teasing, my dear brother. I know all that. Anyway, Goebbels said that if he ever had the power he'd make me pay heavily for it all. They'll do anything to

---

*\*Sturmabteilung*: a paramilitary wing of the Nazi Party.

exterminate the Jews. And it doesn't make any difference that you and I aren't religious, or even believers, just like all our brothers and sisters. As far as they're concerned, a Jew is a Jew, or to use their elegant vocabulary, 'vermin is vermin.' So even though we don't wear skullcaps or side-curls, we're no less Jewish than our dear parents. They'll destroy us."

"Do you think that's possible?"

"Hitler's a thug," Uncle Lion replies, "a former prisoner, a schemer leading a band of good-for-nothings. They'll do anything. They're like the barons in the Middle Ages wanting to add another kingdom to their land. They want castles, gold and serfs. Like the barons, they'll use the Jews to whip up hatred in the masses, who are still just as superstitious as in those days."

"Which is the gist of your novel," says my father.

"Which is selling better than *Mein Kampf*..."

"Neither of them predicts much good news for us in this country," Aunt Marta chips in.

"In any event, I don't know whether your rat of a neighbor will read my next book, but I'll get him all right. I'll quote from memory what I wrote this morning and you can tell me whether you know who I'm talking about."

I'm happy listening. The words slide over me, slipping away, escaping, but I catch them.

Uncle Lion's voice is like music, a tune I can hold:

" 'When he spoke in public his voice became squeaky, verging on hysteria, the words springing effortlessly from his mouth with its thin pale lips. He accompanied his speeches with sweeping hand movements like fly fishers. He was easy to understand, his opinions were perfect topics of conversation for commenting on everyday life. The root of evil was moneylending, the Jews and the Pope. An international cabal of Jewish financiers was destroying the German population, as tuberculosis bacteria would healthy lungs. All would be well and everything would fall into place once the parasites were eliminated. When the Kutzner machine stopped talking, his thin lips and little black mustache, his graying hair plastered onto his head, which was almost completely flat at the back, made him look like an empty mask. But the moment he opened his mouth again, his face came eerily to life with an almost hysterical intensity, his nose tipped upwards, and he rekindled life and energy in those around him. News of Rupert Kutzner's eloquence spread; he had found a way forward, with all the genius of simplicity, and it consisted in purifying public life and restoring it to its most basic principles. Larger and larger crowds came to listen to him, attentively, approvingly. A printer published a confidential paper dedicated entirely to Kutzner's ideas. In print, these ideas looked more muddled. But they had the advantage of reminding readers of the powerful impression the man made when he rode the tide of his own oratory. More and more people came to the Zum Gaisgarten restaurant. The manager, the printer, the boxer and two drivers set up a political party, the Real Germans, which now no longer referred to Kutzner as a machine, but as a political writer.' " Uncle Lion paused, then asked, "So, what do you think?"

"Well," said my father, "you're not pulling your punches!"

"When I think that at one time, before your neighbor was sent to prison, he would treat me to a 'Herr Doctor' at Munich's Hofgarten Café, where we often went with Bertolt Brecht!" exclaimed Uncle Lion. "I wonder what Dr. Freud would make of it. I slipped him into my novel, actually; he'll be amused. Incidentally, I've brought Bertolt's new opera libretto, *The Threepenny Opera*. I came up with the title! It's good, wouldn't you say? He came to see me in the hospital, after my operation, and I saved him from the terrible titles he was contemplating! It's a sellout at the Theater am Schiffbauerdamm in Berlin."

As I crouch under the table, the conversation makes a sort of purring sound overhead. The words and names jumble together, always the same ones: "Jew," "war," "Hitler."

What I really want is to see Aunt Marta's new car. It's far more impressive than Herr Hitler's. I'd like to block my ears now. I can hear them through the table, still talking about the same old things. Uncle Lion makes jokes, but Papa has stopped laughing. His voice is tired.

I eventually came out of hiding and sat on the sofa. I wanted to go to sleep but made myself stay awake. After dinner, my mother sat at the piano and sight-read the libretto Uncle Lion had brought. She hummed a little as she played. It was the story of some very poor people, like the beggars who knocked on our door the other day.

My father, Uncle Lion and Aunt Marta stood around her. I went over to them. Uncle Lion looked sad. My father said I must go to bed, and took me to my room. While he hugged me goodnight I kept listening to Mama's voice and the piano. The song was about England. England's an island, Papa explained. I pictured a country floating on the sea, and fell asleep.

■ ■ ■

My father didn't go to the office this morning. He put on his dressing gown, the one he wears when he edits manuscripts at home. But he's not working now: my mother asked him to stay to look after me because she and Rosie have gone to take care of Aunt Bobbie, who's been ill for several days. Aunt Bobbie's not really my aunt, she's our upstairs neighbor, and she owns the building, which she inherited from her parents. She's lived here since she was little, like me, and like Mama. They played together as children, and their parents were friends before them. Aunt Bobbie lets out rooms to lodgers: when new ones come she introduces them to me, and they come to say goodbye to me when they leave. Rosie and I have been praying to Jesus that she won't die. I pray her heart will keep beating because I know that's how you live. In case that prayer isn't answered, I pray Aunt Bobbie will go up to heaven and will be happy there with her parents. She adored her parents. She'll go to paradise, where we'll all meet again someday. I don't want my parents to die. And I don't ever want to die myself. I often think

about that in bed at night. I know it's impossible. But
maybe, in my case...


Aunt Bobbie's feeling better. Her sister Friedl visits her
every day and this morning she suggested the rest of us
could have a picnic in the country now that Bobbie's out
of danger. My mother thought it a very good idea: I was
pale and the fresh air would do me good. She wasn't happy
leaving Aunt Bobbie at home alone, though, so she offered
to stay with her. My father said he was too busy for a
picnic, he had manuscripts to read and texts to edit, but
when he realized Mama was getting annoyed he agreed to
the outing. Mama announced that she would prepare the
picnic herself while Rosie dressed me for the country and
Papa got himself ready. Friedl winked at me. She knows
I love her car. When she comes to see Bobbie she parks
on the street outside and sounds her horn so I can see her
through the window. She said her daughter would be coming too. I did try not to blush. I often wonder whether people can hear what I'm thinking. I hope not. I don't think
they can, otherwise I'd hear what's going on in their heads.
I'd like to have that gift, reading other people's thoughts,
seeing what they see, but most of all, I don't want anyone
to know that I think Friedl's daughter is very pretty. Her
name's Arabella, she's five, like me, with green eyes and
blond hair. She has a tiny thin nose, she always seems to be
well behaved, and when she smiles I know I go red.

The roof is open. I'm in the back with Arabella, and
Friedl is driving. My father's up front, wearing a white

suit, white vest, white shirt and a white hat that he holds with one hand to stop it blowing away. There's a lovely smell of warm leather. I burned my thighs slightly when I sat down on the sunbaked seats. Arabella has lowered the armrest between us. The sky is blue, striped with fine white lines like trails of cotton wool. The car makes a lovely noise and bounces along the road. There are holes and bumps, and a cloud of dust billows behind us. Friedl sounds the horn when we overtake bicycles or carts or farm laborers pushing barrows full of fruit and vegetables. I put out my arm, reaching out my hand like the wing of an airplane and swinging it up and down. I imagine I'm flying.

We played rock-paper-scissors, twenty questions and charades, we sang as we watched the countryside go by, and I fell asleep. When I woke we were on the shores of Lake Starnberg, parked up beside a cross. My father told us to get out of the car and before we were allowed to go play he gave us a history lesson. History doesn't mean "his story," and it's not a story anyway: it's real things that happened a long time ago. Other stories are the exact opposite: they're completely invented.

Papa showed us the cross and a small church right behind it. He explained that the cross and the chapel were erected in memory of King Ludwig II, who died here, looking out to Empress Sissi's castle, which we could see on the other side of the lake. Arabella asked whether it was in the days of knights. My father said it wasn't as long ago as that because it was in his own lifetime. He told us about the king, said he was called Ludwig like him—which made me smile—and was nicknamed the "Mad King." That made Arabella and me laugh so much! He told us how romantic the king was, miming out the meaning of the word on bended knee before Friedl, gesticulating comically as if he were the Mad King and Friedl the princess who didn't love him. Using a stick he found on the ground, he pretended to drive a dagger into his heart, and slumped onto his side. Arabella and I ran over to him, giggling, prodding him to bring him back to life. Papa told us how Ludwig II believed he had special, very pure blood flowing in his veins. Papa's face grew more serious when he explained that this was nonsense, everyone has the same blood. Friedl said all that matters is the color of our souls. Some are described as dark and others beautiful, pure and noble, the souls of princes, like mine—or princesses, like Arabella's. Then Papa told us how the Mad King had built a fairy-tale castle, with such tall pointy towers that they pierced the clouds. We'll go see it this summer, when we go for our vacation with Uncle Heinrich, my mother's brother who has a house on the other side of the lake, opposite the Mad King's fortress.

Friedl took the food from the trunk of the car. She opened a wicker basket with a whole set of tableware in it. It was magnificent. I wished she didn't have to unfasten the plates, glasses and napkins, or the bread and cold meats. Everything was strapped in its own place. It looked like a doll's tea set. We laid it all out on a colorful tablecloth. My father took a parasol as white as his suit and drove it into the ground. Mama and Rosie had packed up a real feast, which Friedl and Papa spread out before us: hard-boiled eggs, cold chicken, mayonnaise, sausages, potato salad...we demolished the lot.

For dessert, Friedl sliced up peaches for us and sprinkled them with sugar. We had to use our forks but I couldn't pick up the last pink-tinged granules of sugar. I was allowed to let them melt on my tongue. Friedl was worried I'd stain the white lace napkins; she cleaned up my face with water from the lake. After the meal we put on our woolen swimming things and went to play on the shore, getting only our hands, feet and faces wet because Arabella and I couldn't swim. We skipped stones. I couldn't get them to bounce on the surface, one after the other they vanished without a ripple. My father's, on the other hand, seemed to spring off into infinity. They were like aquatic grasshoppers. Yachts glided along the horizon, their pointed, ballooning sails looking like the necks of the swans at the park, and I fell asleep holding Arabella's hand.

When we woke everything had been cleared away. We said goodbye to the lake, climbed into the car and set off. Dark trees masked a mauve sky. I was aware of jolting on the road surface, the sound of the door opening, Papa's arms carrying me, Mama's lips on my cheek, my clothes sliding off, crisp pajamas, cold sheets, and I went back to sleep.

■ ■ ■

Arabella doesn't visit anymore. I miss her.

Aunt Bobbie has recovered. Her friend der Herzog, Luitpold of Bavaria, came to let us know. He's in my father's study and I'm spying on them. They make me  laugh: they're standing talking to each other earnestly, swaying back and forth, rolling onto the balls of their feet and then their heels, like puppets. The duke is grimacing to stop his monocle falling out. They take books from the shelves, open them, leaf through them, and sometimes they just put them back without saying anything. My father is at the top of his library steps reaching for a large book that's been put away too high up for him. My mother brings in coffee, and I come out of hiding to ask whether I can dunk a sugar lump. They talk about Friedl and her husband. I can see the duke doesn't like the man. He says the fellow "admires Hitler," our neighbor, but doesn't expand on this. I don't like anyone criticizing Friedl, and I so want to see Arabella again. I wonder whether we can get married someday, Arabella and I. Or perhaps we won't be allowed to because I'm Jewish and she isn't. I think it might be possible; my father had another wife before my mother, and she wasn't Jewish. They had a child together, Dorle, my beloved sister; she's twelve and she sometimes comes to live at our house.

■ ■ ■

The weather's getting hotter and hotter. The days are long. They're stretching out, and so am I because I'm growing. It will soon be summer. I can't wait for our vacation at Uncle Heinrich's house, where I hope we can visit the Mad King's castle. Rosie's been packing our bags since the start of the week. She folds the laundry and arranges it in piles that she separates and puts away, some in the drawers of the dresser in my bedroom, others in the suit-cases and trunks waiting side by side in the corridor, lined up like soldiers. Mama checks, rummages, dismantles the piles of clothes, puts them together again, unfolds things and folds them back up, hesitates, chooses, changes her mind. And when Papa comes home from work in the eve-ning, she discusses the packing with him, asking his opin-ion. I get the feeling he answers without really hearing her. Like when I'm asleep and Mama or Rosie talks to me: I can hear their voices but I keep on dreaming.

■ ■ ■

I saw Uncle Heinrich park under my window this morn-ing. The car door opened, he stepped out and lit a cig-arette, watching the building opposite the whole time. The lights were on upstairs in Hitler's house. But the sun was already up. I could see a shadow moving behind the gray curtains. I wondered whether Hitler could see me and whether he knew I was going away on vacation. The doorbell startled me, and suddenly Uncle Heinrich was there. I ran to kiss him. Everyone was in a good mood. We took the suitcases downstairs and tied them to the roof-rack. Rosie, who isn't coming on vacation with us, kissed me and hugged me so tightly I couldn't breathe. Everyone laughed at me and, as usual, I blushed. Then we set off.

We've been traveling for hours. Uncle Heinrich is telling us that Richard Strauss, whom he works for, is writing an opera that will be called *Arabella*. I know who Richard Strauss is. There's a piece I know because Mama sings it to me, *Salome*. One evening she performed the "Dance of the Seven Veils" when she was dressed up as a princess for a masked ball. She promised me that when I'm a big boy we'll go to see it at the opera, next to Hitler's house. They're all smoking in the car and it makes me feel sick. Uncle Heinrich is saying Richard Strauss loves money and has a little palace in the mountains, at Garmisch in the Alps, looking out over the Zugspitze.

"That old lunatic is utterly tireless," Uncle Heinrich says. "When he's not composing, he has a constant stream of family coming and going, musicians come to stay in his vast villa, and he sings and plays the piano for them, and he also loves conducting other people's operas, Mozart's *Così fan tutte* and Wagner's *Tristan*. He's like a metronome, unstoppable, right hand in the air, baton extended, left hand in his pocket. Never seen anything like it. At sixty-five he has more energy than his singers. He goes skating sometimes when the lakes freeze over. He's a forbidding-looking man but you should see him playing skat! There's no holding him!"

Mama explains that skat's a card game.

"And what are his political leanings?" my father asks.

"He's certainly not a Nazi," Uncle Heinrich replies. "In fact, his son Franz has just married the ravishing Alice Grab, who, like us, my dear brother-in-law, is a noble descendant of Abraham. She's the daughter of Emanuel von Grab, a Czech industrialist and an old friend."

"Jews, Nazis...can't you talk about something else, for goodness' sake!" Mama pleads irritably. "You'll frighten Edgar."

I fall asleep. I'm not frightened. In my dream I'm the Red Baron. I'm Manfred von Richthofen, a flying ace. I'm flying a three-winged Fokker Dr1. My plane is red with a large German cross painted on the tail. I've already shot down eighty enemy planes. I attack the French, pursue the English and drive off the Canadians and Americans. I pepper them with machine-gun fire. My enemies' planes nose-dive and crash, and the pilots parachute down. I chase the RAF ace Arthur Roy Brown through the clouds. With every victory I draw a cross on my cockpit. I'm wearing a leather helmet and big goggles. I fly over the Alps and Richard Strauss's house. A little girl performs the "Dance of the Seven Veils" for me. She sings. I can smell her perfume, it's blue, I hear a horn sounding, and I'm not sure whether I'm still dreaming.

I wake in a large wood-paneled bedroom. I get up and open the curtains. There's a big gray lake and the sky's gray too, with a hint of pink on the horizon mingling with the color of the lake. In the mountains in the distance I see a castle with towers tapering up into the clouds. The Mad King's castle. I realize we must have arrived at Uncle Heinrich's house. I open the bedroom door and go downstairs. Uncle Heinrich is in the large drawing room, wearing a silk dressing gown over a striped shirt and a beautiful scarf. I can hear music, and spot the gramophone. It's a contraption with a sort of trumpet, or rather a kind of large shell, and the music comes out of there.

A black record is spinning on the turntable. The "Dance
of the Seven Veils" again. I recognize it immediately and
Uncle Heinrich says I have a musical ear. Mama and
Papa come in and I run to kiss them. Uncle Heinrich tells
them I have a gift for music and I can tell they're pleased.
But I'd rather be a flying ace.

We've been on vacation for a long time now. I'd like to
stay here my whole life. It's better than Munich. We play
a board game called the Game of the Goose in the large
drawing room. We play croquet in the garden, using
mallets to strike different-colored wooden balls that
roll through arches planted in the soft grass. We look
for four-leaf clovers. One afternoon my mother read
my palm and told me I'd live to at least a hundred. That
would be 2024. We go down to the lake every day to
swim, except I don't because I can't swim yet. I'm frightened I'll drown like the Mad King. I stay playing with
my little boats on the shore, and Mama watches me, then
we go back up to the house for lunch. In the afternoon
I have to take a nap. I'm not sleepy, I lie there thinking,
looking at the things in my bedroom, wondering whether
they can see me, then I fall asleep. My father and Uncle
Heinrich work in Munich during the week and join us
on Friday. They never stop talking about the Nazis and
our neighbor Hitler, and I've had enough of it, it's no fun.
And Mama definitely agrees with me about that!

■ ■ ■

That vacation was a long time ago. I'm a big boy now. When we came home Rosie's eyes were red and shiny. I thought she was going to cry. I told her not to be sad, and she said she had tears in her eyes because she was happy to see me again. I was touched.

The next day I noticed Herr Hitler was there. He'd come home too. Did he go for a vacation with his family? Did they have picnics?

The telephone didn't stop ringing all day. Papa came home from the office early with a pile of newspapers under his arm. Uncle Heinrich stopped by the house, looking worried. I didn't dare say hello to him because he looked so sad. In the evening, after I'd had my bath and my supper, Papa explained that Uncle Heinrich had lost almost all his money, and would have to sell the villa by the lake. I thought about our swimming trips, the gramophone, our games of croquet, the Mad King's castle, four-leaf clovers and my wood-paneled bedroom. I asked Papa whether it was something to do with this "Black Thursday" I'd heard Uncle Heinrich talking about.

"Yes," he said with a smile. "That's what they're calling yesterday because it was like a day of mourning for people who lost all their savings, sometimes their homes."

I asked whether we had been ruined. He kissed me and laughed: their wealth was their little boy, and no one could take that away from them.

*While the Goddess of Suffering took me in her arms, often threatening to crush me, my will to resistance grew, and in the end this will was victorious.*

*I owe it to that period that I grew hard and am still capable of being hard. And even more, I exalt it for tearing me away from the hollowness of comfortable life; for drawing the mother's darling out of his soft downy bed and giving him "Dame Care" for a new mother; for hurling me, despite all resistance, into a world of misery and poverty, thus making me acquainted with those for whom I was later to fight.*

—ADOLF HITLER, *MEIN KAMPF*, ON HIS TROUBLES

AS A YOUNG ARTIST IN VIENNA

Snowflakes have been dancing in the sky since this morning. We can't see the building opposite. Santa Claus came a few days ago. I guess he came in his sleigh. He left me masses of presents again, but I'm bored because I'm all alone. I wish I had a real brother or sister at home with me every day. My sister, Dorle, came for Christmas. She and her mother came from Berlin by train. I watched from my window as they stepped out of the taxi laden with suitcases and presents. I thought the presents must be for me. Strangely, by the time they reached our floor the presents had disappeared! I was disappointed although I tried not to show it. Luckily we all had lots of presents under the tree the next morning, and some of them looked peculiarly like the parcels I'd seen Dorle and her mother carrying the day before.

Dorle's mother is called Lilly. I call her Aunt Lilly. She and my mother have fun teasing Papa. They say he's lazy and scatterbrained and doesn't know how to dress. It makes him laugh. Me too. We all had lunch together, then Aunt Lilly left and Dorle unpacked her bags in my bedroom. I love it when she lives at our house. I watched everything. She had a bag full of books with no pictures as well as magazines.

During her stay Dorle liked to read the *Berliner Illustrierte Zeitung*, which my father keeps protectively in his study. I looked through it with her and asked questions. I wasn't allowed to touch the pages in case I dirtied them or tore them, so she turned them. She knew all the movie actresses. Marlene Dietrich was the most beautiful. Dorle dressed up as her sometimes: she put on lipstick, a hat of my father's, a little jacket and no pants. Just panty hose. She sang, "*Ich bin von Kopf bis Fuß auf liebe eingestellt*" (I'm made for love from head to toe).

Dorle read me an article about the Vampire of Düsseldorf, a criminal who prowls the city by night and kills children. He offers them candy and carries them away, and their bodies are found hidden later. He's killed dozens of children. He stabs them and strangles them, and the police haven't managed to find him. No one knows who he is. The people of Düsseldorf all suspect their neighbors and won't let their children out. Even in Munich people are advised to keep an eye on their little ones. Mama scolded Dorle and told me not to believe such stories. But I know newspapers tell the truth and Dorle never lies. Now I'm frightened the Vampire of Düsseldorf will come to Munich.

Dorle showed me photographs of beggars but I didn't recognize the ones who came to our house. She told me there were even more of them in Berlin, especially since Black Thursday. On one page I recognized our neighbor Adolf Hitler. I pointed through the window to show Dorle where he lives.

Dorle read magazines to me all week. She told me she'd like to be an actress and live in America, in Hollywood. She told me about her favorite films. When she was little like me, her favorite actor was Charlie Chaplin. She showed me a picture. I thought he looked like Hitler. They have the same little mustache. In the photo, Charlie Chaplin was dressed as a beggar. He was sitting beside a child my age. Dorle told me that in Hollywood you could be an actor from as young as five, and that this child actor, Jackie Coogan, was richer than his parents by the time he was seven. I'll be seven soon myself. Then she showed me *Mickey Mouse*, a comic strip. Mickey is a black and white mouse who stands on his hind legs, walks down the street and goes to the movies. Everything in the book is in color except for Mickey Mouse, as if the cartoonist forgot to color him in. I asked my mother to take me to the movies. I want to see Charlie Chaplin. I want to watch cartoons. I want to see Mickey Mouse. She promised me we'd go soon.

■ ■ ■

When we went for our walk yesterday we passed his house. Dorle wanted to see the name Adolf Hitler on the door. The guard stared at her insistently; Rosie took her hand and hurried away. Farther up the street she told Dorle she shouldn't have looked.

"It's not forbidden," Dorle replied tartly. "And anyway, his name isn't written on the door. It says 'Winter,' not 'Hitler'!"

It was the first time I'd seen a child talk back to an adult. Rosie didn't say anything. The guard was watching us. Rosie turned away and we walked on. It was cold, it was still snowing. Passersby walked carefully so as not to fall.

We were meeting my father at the Fürstenhof Café. We waited for the tram on the other side of the street, under the watchful eye of the man outside Hitler's house. I was relieved to hear the sound of wheels on the metal rails snaking along the cobbled street. The driver rang his bell. We stepped back to let passengers off, and then we climbed in. Everyone in the car was smoking, and we huddled in tight. Dorle wanted to sit on one of the black benches but a stern-faced Rosie told her to leave the seats for grown-ups.

We alighted just opposite the café. It has a huge room and I'm always afraid I'll be trodden underfoot there. The waiters run backward and forward with trays laden with pints of beer, holding them above their heads. My father was sitting at the back, with his brother the veteran, my soldier uncle, Berthold. Papa told Rosie she could go for a little walk, and he ordered us our favorite snack. Dorle and I always have the same thing: chocolate ice cream smothered with whipped cream and molten chocolate. Dorle launched straight into telling them that Hitler had a false name on his door. But Papa knew that already.

"Yes, yes, I know," he said. "It's his cleaner's name. He's worried people will come and bother him. He's a coward."

"But, Luidgie," said Uncle Berthold, "you know perfectly well he lived through the trenches like me. Why would he be afraid of his own shadow? He just doesn't want to be pestered by all those women who keep pursuing him."

"Oh yes, the trenches! He moans about them all the way through his tedious doorstop, *Mein Kampf*. He wails. Laments. Cries. Shrieks. You can picture him rolling on the floor like a baby as he writes the book. He resents the whole world, he really does. The French, the generals, his corporal, the Jews, the rats…Besides, he doesn't make any distinction between those last two categories—because, oh yes, according to him, anyone who practices the Jewish religion is quite simply a different species. A subspecies, he says. A bit like 'vermin,' to use one of his writerly terms. Charming, wouldn't you say? And what do we do to vermin? I'll leave you to work that out."

"Yes, Hitler's a bastard. But the world's in a mess, you know. What will happen here? What will become of us? What future is there for Germany? We need to do *something*!"

"But can't you see what Hitler's like?" my father retorts. "He hates the Jews, he hates the whole world, and so do all his cronies. He's disturbed, bitter, paranoid, violent and—most of all—dangerous. Did you know Lion's publishing a book about him in a few days' time? *Success*, it charts the rise of a wretch just like him. It's very funny.

"He describes him as a sort of hysteric who rants nineteen to the dozen. In his last book, *Jud Süß*, Lion was already talking about upstarts in the past who whipped up the crowds to massacre our ancestors in our country. It's the only book beating *Mein Kampf* hands down in terms of sales. *Success* should make even more of a stir because it so obviously caricatures him. Lion wants Hitler's readers to see that this failed artist is really a usurper and, more importantly, a very dangerous character who's dragging us back several centuries."

"Oh, come on, Lion's got too much imagination," Berthold protested. "This isn't the Middle Ages, after all. People travel. You can get to Rome or Paris overnight. Even Hitler wasn't born in a cave. He admires Wagner and he's read the great philosophers. Actually, I thought you knew him when you were younger…"

"Knew? That's a strong word. He hung around the area. We came across each other. But we never exchanged a word. He was the one who came to say hello to Lion and Bertolt Brecht at the Café Stefanie one time. That was before he got so frenzied, before he tried his putsch in 1924. In fact, the only good thing about that putsch business was that he lost sixteen of his henchmen and was condemned to six years in prison. To think he was let out on parole after just nine months, what a blunder! As if someone like that could be taken at their word. Did you know he pledged to keep out of politics? If his sentence had been properly implemented he wouldn't have come out of prison till last year. We need only have applied the law and we'd have been rid of him and his party. Now he knows how to go about it. He doesn't put himself in the firing line anymore. He stays on the brink of legitimacy, hiding behind his curtains in his apartment. He's even taken to looking like his new targets, the lesser bourgeoisie who are so terrified of losing everything and finding themselves on the street. He's just as bourgeois as the next man. He's just like me. Like any of us. He lives in the same neighborhood, wears the same suits and listens to the same music. But that's only his outward appearance, a disguise. In the shadows his sidekicks have changed none of their methods or their objectives. Hitler's our neighbor but he's a dangerous man. Do you know he now likes to be called the 'King of Munich'?"

"Well, his party's nothing now," Berthold said dismissively. "They'll be slaughtered at the elections."

"Do you think? I can tell you plenty of people go past here in the street every day saluting him with their outstretched arms, like gladiators before a Roman emperor. We can see him from our drawing room, watching from his balcony, admiring this crowd of thugs prostrating themselves before him and cheering him like some demigod. He's perfectly capable of getting everyone on the planet to wear togas again and bring back slavery. He must dream about that! And so must his troops! I see them getting drunk every evening in brasseries, around the back of where we live, celebrating their patron saint's famous failed putsch, toasting their sixteen martyrs and dreaming of success next time. Anyone would think we've rewound the clock several centuries. Anyone would think they were tribes of warriors, savages and sadists. The SA dress up like bogus soldiers and terrorize people in the street, men, women, children, the elderly. They wander about, often drunk, bellowing that they're pure-blooded superhumans, only ever operating in groups, herds, packs. Oh, if they take power, like their barbaric acolytes in Italy, I wouldn't give our dear democracy long, nor our wonderful republic, which, alas, lets these carnivores roam free. Yes, they're preparing for carnage."

"What? If they came to power?" my uncle asked, amazed. "But that's impossible! They got less than three percent in the last election. The country's far too republican to vote for them. Since the war there are nothing but pacifists, pen-pushers, civil servants, leftists, and Communists, and the only word on their lips is 'republic,' as if that could feed the millions of workers laid off by the Treaty of Versailles and this wretched Black Thursday brought on by bankers in New York, London and Paris...Do you know unemployment has risen tenfold in the last year? There are now five million out of work. And all our leaders can think of is getting rid of business charges and reducing benefits for individuals. And look at the results! *That*'s not your neighbor's fault, at least!"

"Don't start that again..."

"Well, all right," Berthold seemed to concede, but immediately started again. "Still, what I wanted to say was that if Hitler were elected to power, he wouldn't do any worse than those other incompetents, these leftists who range from left-of-center to extreme left, these good-for-nothings in government at the moment. Not to mention giving a good kick up the backside to all the privileged who are stuffing their faces while the people are suffering."

"What about the Jews?" my father asked. "What do you think he would do with the Jews? And the Gypsies? The Communists, trade unionists, anyone who doesn't share his views? What does he have planned for them?"

"It's bluster, just words, youthful talk, blurted out in anger, in prison. Besides, it's been dropped from his agenda. Do you remember my friend Weiss Ferdl?" Berthold asked.

"You mean the actor? You know him?"

"Yes, we fought together," explained my uncle, then he paused briefly before continuing. "Well, so, he knows Hitler. He told me he isn't at all the man we think he

37

is. In fact, Weiss mentioned me to him, saying I'm living proof that Jews aren't cowards. Apparently Hitler agreed. Well, he said, 'that's the exception that proves the rule.' But that was a quip. He's quite a wit. Anyway, all that talk is misinformation, you know. The French have a lot of influence, the Americans too. And the British also. Look at Italy, Mussolini's been in power for nearly ten years. I can assure you their country's doing much better. Democracy has its weaknesses too. Denigrating anything that challenges it, among other things."

"Do you think they'll spare you, then?" my father seemed to challenge him. "Have you actually read *Mein Kampf*?"

One of the waiters dropped his tray. We heard the glasses break on the floor. Customers applauded. I looked up from my delicious ice cream. Smoke hung in the air, stinging my eyes as I scanned the room. I dove back into my ice-cream glass, so deep I could hear my breathing inside it.

"I bought it like everyone else," said my uncle. "But I have to admit I haven't read it. Well, not all of it, just a few pages, about the war."

"You should read it. It's more explicit than you think. I promise you."

"Maybe," Uncle Berthold said slowly. "But look at the state the country's in. Oh, if only we'd been able to fight for a few more months, instead of giving in like that and surrendering everything to our enemies who are now infiltrating us and exploiting us!"

"You should get yourself a job, and a wife. You should—"

"Stop, please," my uncle said, holding up one hand. "I don't tell you how to live your life. Let's talk about something else..."

Night was falling outside. I could hear the two of them talking but wasn't listening to them. Voices reverberated around the room, making a lot of noise. A dulled sound, like when I put my ears underwater in the bath. I could hear glasses, chairs grating, car horns outside, and people calling to waiters.

"Are you dreaming, Bürschi?" asked my uncle, startling me. I climbed onto his lap. My father and mother often criticize him, but I think he's kind. And incredibly brave. He fought in the war! I adore him.

"Did *you* know Hitler?" I asked. "Were you in the trenches with him? Was he your friend?"

"My friend? Are you crazy? My enemy, you mean! A man like that deserved not to come back from the battle-field. You listen to me, Bürschi, your neighbor looks like any other man, but the most cowardly of maniacs is hiding behind that mustache. Your father's right."

My father smiled. He paid the check and we stood up. Rosie was waiting for us outside. We kissed my uncle goodbye and went home.

Standing in front of our house, we all looked up. I saw Adolf Hitler's silhouette in the window. He seemed very small. He was looking far into the distance. We went upstairs in silence.

■ ■ ■

Our cousins the Bernheimers have invited us to spend the day with them today. They've sent their car over, an American model. It's a red Packard with white-edged tires and a running board along the sides that scrolls up like a wave over the wheels. Amesmeyer, the driver, is wearing a dark uniform with gold buttons. His black peaked cap matches the car, with its white edging, red stitching and a visor as shiny as the mirrors. Amesmeyer takes the roof down and I feel like a prince being transported in the back of a carriage. He starts up the engine. Off we go. Gliding. I see Hitler's Mercedes, which looks smaller now. Is he at the window? The building disappears behind us.

Amesmeyer opens the door of the Packard for us and we step out. The Bernheimers' house is a private mansion; it feels like arriving at a hotel. We ring the doorbell and a butler opens it, letting us into the huge hall adorned with paintings the size of windows. Another servant, dressed in a tailcoat and gray pants, helps us off with our coats and takes them to a room I've never seen. I always feel a little awkward because I prefer taking off my coat myself. No hope of that, he's always faster than me. He calls me Herr Edgar.

My cousin Ingrid is here, standing waiting for me in the hall with her blond hair held back by a gold barrette.

She reaches for my hand and takes me off to play. Her bedroom, a space barely smaller than our whole apartment, is furnished like a miniature palace, with a princess bed and a huge doll's house we can go inside. We play there all day, dreaming up different worlds for ourselves: she's a queen and I'm a knight, I'm a fishmonger, she's a housewife. By four o'clock we're hungry. It's time for afternoon tea. We go out into the garden to get to the kitchen on the other side of the house. There we find delicious treats carefully lined up on silver trays. I just love the *Bündnerfleisch* and the tiny sausages you dip in mustard. Ingrid's nanny has prepared fruit juices for us, orange, and grenadine all the way from Paris. In the drawing room, bearskins are draped over red sofas the size of the boats we take on the lakes in summer. Ingrid's mother is playing a grand piano.

We often go to the Bernheimers'. We celebrated Christmas with them one time. I was dressed like a grown-up with a little tuxedo and patent shoes. The women wore satin gloves and hats decorated with feathers. Their faces were half hidden behind black nets, through which everything sparkled: their heavily made-up eyes, the red of their lips and their pearly teeth. Guests allowed chambermaids to take their belongings and carry them away carefully: women's coats in fox fur and sable, their husbands' gold-handled canes, top hats and heavy coats, some dark, some brightly colored. Cars filed by outside. I watched their measured dance. Butlers opened the doors to carriages with their gloved hands, revealing the leather interiors in red, almond, gray, black, cream or white. In the drawing room an orchestra played familiar tunes by Mozart, Beethoven, Handel and Bach, and other, more entertaining pieces, jazz and fox-trots. Before we were taken to bed in Ingrid's room, I watched the adults dancing, crisscrossing their knees and arms more and more quickly. Late into the night we heard the sounds of the party and grown-ups laughing. We fell asleep lulled by melodies played on the violin, piano and clarinet.

We're now at the Bernheimers' country house in Oberföring. Their villa is the size of a castle. Our parents are so afraid we'll get lost in the grounds that Ingrid's nanny follows our every move, to the stables and the kitchen garden, into the greenhouses and the orangery, around the maze and onto the tennis court. On our travels we meet the estate's dogs and cats, including an adorable little puppy.


This year we extend our vacation with friends of my parents', the Siegels. They don't have a castle, their house in Munich isn't as large as the Bernheimers' and their chalet in Walchensee is more like a shack than a villa. In the distance along the shores of the lake we can make out stilts where the locals regularly go to haul up their oyster beds, standing in their boats on the green waters. Cows graze unfenced, looking out over the mountainous scenery. But by far the best thing is that they have a daughter my age: Beate. We haven't spent a moment apart all summer. We've watched the sun set every evening, hand in hand, and picked so many daisies in the meadow that there are no more to be found by the end of our stay. We're sorry to say goodbye, but we know we won't be apart long.

Beate lives very close to us, on the other side of the square that runs along the side of Hitler's house.

Since we've been home from our vacation, there's been talk of nothing but politics in the house. Uncle Lion's book has been published. It's in all the bookshops. When we go for our walks, Rosie points it out to me in windows. I feel proud when I see it. The bookseller told us it seems to be selling better than *Mein Kampf*. I know it says bad things about Hitler; I also know our neighbor's a dangerous man. My parents, my grandparents, and Beate's relations too are all saying the same thing: he's a liar and a thief. Even the milkman talked to Rosie about it. He told her Hitler was taking all the milk for the neighborhood so there was less for everyone else. My mother was furious. According to my father, the milkman was wrong because no one can requisition their neighbors' milk. He also said that Hitler couldn't single-handedly drink the usual milk consumption of several families. Otherwise it would be good news because it would kill him!

He's right in front of us, outside his building. We've stopped in our tracks. Rosie is stock-still. I can see he's cut himself shaving, as my father sometimes does. He has blue eyes. I didn't know that. You can't see that in photos.

I thought his eyes were completely black. I've never seen him so close up. He has hairs in his nose, and a few in his ears. He's shorter than I thought. Shorter than my father. Shorter than Rosie. Passersby stop, like us. He looks at me. I should look away. But I can't. I stare at him. Maybe I should smile? I'm his neighbor, after all! Does he recognize me? Does he know I watch him from my bedroom? Can he see inside our house? Does he watch us eating in the dining room? Does he know I'm Jewish? I don't want him to hate me. Or my father. Or my mother. Are people looking at me? He's climbed into a dark car, black as night, its lines as hard as stone.

■ ■ ■

On the way home from the park with Rosie, I ran along the sidewalk, rolling my hoop ahead of me with little nudges of the stick. Uncle Lion was at home when we reached the house. I've come to sit on the floor in the sunshine in the drawing room, to listen to what they're saying. My mother looks worried, my father serious. Only Uncle Lion is still smiling. They're all looking at a newspaper open on the coffee table.

"Look what they're doing, it's disgusting," says my father.

There's an illustration of a great fat man wearing a bow tie; he has a big nose and eyebrows like bushes.

"Don't get in a state about nothing," says Uncle Lion. "Wait till you see the review by Herr Goebbels himself, the newspaper chief and a regular guest at your neighbor's table. He says they'll make me pay when they're in power. What do they mean by that? He doesn't say. Probably because it's not likely to be legal. A public lynching? Murder? Torture? There's no knowing what torments the Nazis will dream up for those they despise, in other words nine tenths of the planet."

"Could they ever come to power?" my mother asks.

"I don't know," Uncle Lion sighs. "Goebbels certainly managed to get himself elected to the Reichstag. Do you know what he said? That he and the eleven other Nazi congressmen were infiltrating the Reichstag like wolves in a sheepfold. The Fascists had no trouble taking power completely in Italy. The elections are in a month, in September. Everyone's expecting them to improve on their last performance. They had only a 3 percent share of the vote three years ago. But unemployment has gone through the roof since then. The Wall Street crash is still casting its long shadow over us. German companies can't sell anything anymore, they're running out of cash. The banks have stopped lending, and their customers are going bankrupt one after another. People are desperate. Because Hitler and his gang have never been in power, they're being credited with every virtue. Well, let's say that some people believe—or hope—that things would be better with them in power, given that their leader says so with such conviction. And the culprits have been identified. The Jews. Of course. Just like in the past, in Rome, in the Middle Ages, the Renaissance. They've started all over again."

"You're exaggerating," says my mother.

"I can promise you I'm not. There are things they'll say to everyone, and then there's what they say among themselves. I read everything they publish. And it never changes. It's obsessive. All they talk about is Jews, foreigners, bankers, saying the world would be a better place without them, of course."

■ ■ ■

One day my parents went out to vote. They didn't take me with them. When they came back, they were in a good mood.

At breakfast the next day they didn't speak at all. They read the newspaper. Rosie was quiet too. I asked her whether Adolf Hitler had won. She said he hadn't, but he hadn't lost either. He took 18 percent of the vote. This means that out in the street, one in five people voted for him, as if one person in our household had voted for the Nazis, and so on in every house. Did Rosie vote for him? She shrugged her shoulders wistfully. She'd voted for the Communists, and only one person in ten had done that.

"The Communists wanted to share everything," she said, "they wanted equality. In the past they fought for workers to have a day of rest on Sundays. Everyone's forgotten that. Now people are happier voting for Hitler, who's never done a day's work in his life."

I've decided to be a Communist when I grow up.

1931

*In this period my eyes were opened to two menaces of which I had previously scarcely known the names, and whose terrible importance for the existence of the German people I certainly did not understand: Marxism and Jewry.*

—ADOLF HITLER, *MEIN KAMPF*, ON HIS EARLY YEARS IN VIENNA

It was my first trip to Dr. Arndt, the dentist. I couldn't wait for the day because I'd lost several baby teeth and the new ones were already coming through, bigger teeth that I'd keep my whole life. I was longing to show them off.

"They'll check you don't have vampire teeth," Rosie teased, imitating the Vampire of Düsseldorf.

My mother and I walked to my appointment, passing the "King of Munich's" house, Prince Regent's Place and the opera house. Mama and I sang together as we walked; sometimes I ran ahead, avoiding puddles and aiming for the joints between paving stones on the sidewalk. Mama opened the front door to the building where the dentist worked. I huddled closer to her, and she stroked my hair and the back of my neck as if she knew what I was thinking. I wanted to leave. We climbed to the first floor, she rang a doorbell and the door was opened by a small woman in a white uniform. Mama gave my name and the stern-looking woman frostily showed us into the waiting room. We weren't alone: a fat lady swimming in a huge fur coat was looking into the mirror of her powder compact and applying makeup. I saw her eyes alight on me, stare at me and then flit back to the Bakelite box. She turned to her neighbor, a small woman dressed in black.

"Who on earth does he think he is?" she said, loudly enough for everyone to hear.

She meant Adolf Hitler, I was sure of it. I'd heard Papa say the only thing he had in common with Adolf Hitler was his dentist—he'd spotted him going into the building one time. So the King of Munich must have been undergoing treatment in the adjoining room that very minute. When the dentist's door opened slightly, we all went quiet, including the woman who talked so loudly. I wondered whether Hitler might have heard her. Or had the padded walls muffled her strident voice? The door stayed ajar a long time. We could hear the dentist talking deferentially to his patient, but all we could see through the opening was a small section of the patient's jacket. I was watching the dentist's wrinkled hand holding the door handle when the door suddenly opened, and we all saw the dentist's face, his white smock and small glasses. And Herr Hitler appeared. He was a short bearded man who looked nothing like our neighbor: he wore a big hat and his hair was arranged into *payot* curls in front of his ears. Not him.

The unknown patient greeted us and left. I thought the woman would get up and go in next. But it was my turn. The dentist kissed Mama's hand, shook mine and showed us in. We each sat in an armchair facing his desk. I was aware of the worn leather under my thighs while he asked Mama questions. He made a note of her answers on a sheet of paper, slowly repeating what she'd said in his deep, gravelly voice. Between his sentences we could hear his pen gliding over the paper. His desk was like my father's: leather topped with a blotter covered in splashes of blue. There was also a small bottle of midnight blue ink, a gleaming paper knife and long silvery scissors that reflected the chandelier hanging from the ceiling. The tick of a clock standing on the mantelpiece before a tall mirror filled the room. I could hear the sounds of car engines and horns from the street. I couldn't help myself looking over to the far side of the room, where a large steel chair stood on a single foot, fitted out with lamps, metallic instruments, mirrors, cables and iron rods. Beyond it, in a dark corner of the office, another leather-padded door opened and a nurse came in. She was wearing a white uniform and a small hat. She looked like Marlene Dietrich.

The dentist asked me to sit in the big chair. Then "Marlene" reclined the chair and smiled at me as I glided backward. She had green eyes and long black eyelashes. I could smell her perfume stealing throughout the room, and felt her sleeve brush past my face. The spotlight went

1931

**49**

on and now all I could see were the facets of glass around the bulb…and the dentist's very pink face. He told me to open my mouth, and eased a cold instrument inside. I felt him lightly tap my teeth, holding my lips open with his fingers. To keep my mind off this, I looked at the nurse. She was smiling at me, her red lips slightly parted, and there was a black dot drawn onto her cheek, just above her mouth. Her teeth were the color of clouds. I wondered whether Hitler thought she was pretty.

The examination was soon over. The dentist said everything was in order and moments later we were back out in the street. On the way home, newspaper salesmen trumpeted that the Vampire of Düsseldorf had been arrested. I would be able to play outside by myself again now. A zeppelin flew across the sky. It disappeared behind a building with a red roof, a typical Munich roof. I thought about the nurse again, about the dentist, and Adolf Hitler.

■ ■ ■

Rosie is in the kitchen reading the paper, which has the whole story of the Vampire, with pictures. Peter Kürten killed at least ten people, only one of them an adult, whom he battered with a hammer. His parents were poor. He had twelve brothers and sisters. Even as a child, he'd drowned two of his friends. As an adult, he stabbed and strangled his other victims. The papers mention that the Vampire was a trade unionist, and Rosie explains that a trade union is a group of workers who come together to get better working conditions in their factory.

"Factory workers have terrible lives," she adds. "They set off for work when it's still dark and come home to go to bed with no dinner. They die before they've had time to grow old. If your father had been a factory worker, he might already be dead and you would never have known him."

I often wonder what it must be like being an orphan. Rosie says that since Black Thursday all the orphanages are full: the poor abandon their babies because they can't feed them. Just before the war, Kürten was sentenced to several years in prison so he avoided going to the front, and as soon as he was out he started strangling children again. This time he should be condemned to death.

The paper also has a photograph of Marshal von Hindenburg. His mustache is shaggy as sheep's wool and curves up his face, and you can see all twenty of his medals. He's a hero, his face even appears on stamps. He's already fought two wars against France. He won the first, in 1870. And if people had listened to him he would have triumphed in the second, the 1914–1918 war. Uncle Berthold told me that the marshal fought all his battles alongside another great strategist, Erich Ludendorff; together they were invincible. They were nicknamed the "Dioskouri," like the twins Castor and Pollux, heroes in my book on Greek mythology. Uncle Berthold showed me color pictures in an illustrated magazine. One was of the two men marching through the streets in their spiked helmets. Another showed them studying military maps on a big table.

"When those two were around, the German army was the strongest in the world," Uncle Berthold sighed.

But when I spoke to Rosie about it, she disagreed: "If it weren't for them, the war would have ended sooner and fewer men would have died. And, anyway, Ludendorff is no better than Hitler, they're both in it for themselves! But at least Hindenburg says it as it is: Hitler's just a lowly corporal from Bohemia."

Hindenburg is eighty-five and he's president of the republic. He hasn't actually been in the post long: he retired after the war and was living peacefully in the country when his former brothers-in-arms came and asked him to come back to power. He was seventy-seven, his wife had just died, he was bored. Rosie's told me she remembers seeing trucks in the street carrying busts of him, followed by men singing about his glorious return and announcing the German army's revenge on the Weimar leftists.

The Weimar Coalition was responsible for signing the peace treaty with France, not giving the "Dioskouri" time to win the war—that's something Uncle Berthold's already told me. Because of them, Germany's sinking into poverty and its war veterans, like my uncle, have never managed to find work again. I felt proud telling Rosie about it, but she claimed my uncle was talking nonsense.

"War never made anyone happy, my little Bürschi," she said. "Weimar isn't a coalition, it's a republic, a democracy, giving people the right to vote. Even women have had the vote since 1918. Thanks to Weimar, Germany is ahead of the rest of the world."

Rosie looked as if she was holding back tears. She told me about her fiancé who never came home from the trenches in Verdun, sliced open by a Frenchman's bayonet. I said I wished I could avenge him.

"No, Bürschi," Rosie replied. "You must never wish for another person to die. The Frenchman died alongside him on the battlefield. One day I'll go and lay a flower for both of them."

1931

■ ■ ■

The Vampire of Düsseldorf has been condemned to death. He's to be beheaded. I'm glad, even though it's wrong to want another person to die. I often think of his victims and of the parents of the children he killed. They must cry day and night. Still, I wouldn't want to see the Vampire having his neck cut by an axe. Newspaper kiosks in the street show pictures of a man skulking in the shadows; they're taken from a film that will soon be released in movie theaters. It's just called *M* and it's the story of the Vampire of Düsseldorf. I won't be allowed to watch it, I know, because they'll say I'm too young. I wish I were a big boy!

■ ■ ■

My father was at home today and he sent me on an errand: to take a book to Thomas Mann. I couldn't wait to go to his house because my parents had often described the gigantic villa filled with astonishing things. Thomas

Mann makes up stories for grown-ups; he writes books by hand on paper, then gives them to an editor—someone who does the same job as my father—who has the book printed on heavy machines.

Rosie went ahead of me along the path that runs the length of the field behind our building. This morning I was dressed like a little sailor, in a sailor suit with a collar, a peacoat and a flat hat. I was allowed to take my butterfly net. The sun was pounding. Luckily, Rosie had taken a flask of water with a few drops of grenadine syrup in it. I didn't spot any butterflies even though the sky was blue and I could see a long way. Bees and flies danced in the sunlight, birds flew in flocks. I was bored. I should have taken my hoop.

At last we arrived at the villa hidden behind a wall of ivy. Rosie rang the doorbell and a man came to let us in. I instantly knew it wasn't Thomas Mann because he was wearing servant's clothes. He took us to the garden and Rosie explained why we were here. Through the villa's windows I saw a man watching us, his hair slicked back over his head. He smoothed his mustache with one hand and held a cigarette in the other. It was hot outside, I could feel sweat running down my back. How cool it must have been inside! I was proud I'd come all that way on foot, and I was still holding the book, which my father had wrapped up in paper and tied with string. I'd promised Papa I'd say hello to Thomas Mann for him. I knew he'd tell me I'd done well. But the servant took the book, thanked us and showed us back to the door without inviting us in. The villa looked to me as if it was enchanted with its huge white stone staircase and its high castle windows. There were children playing on a swing behind the house. Their laughter wafted over to us, carried on the wind. We could hear a river flowing nearby and the buzz of bees…

Why hadn't I been invited in? I felt like crying. Rosie didn't dare ring the bell again, and we went home. On the way back she told me who Thomas Mann was, one of the most famous writers in Germany, like Uncle Lion, who was a friend of his. His books describe the beautiful things in life, they explore the world of children in the old days, of Germany before the Great War. In those days women wore flouncy dresses, and wide hats with flowers on them, and they sheltered from the sun behind parasols. Thomas Mann won the Nobel Prize in Literature: he's the greatest writer in the world.

■ ■ ■

Rosie's reading to me from the newspaper. At six o'clock in the morning yesterday, July 2, 1931, the Vampire of Düsseldorf was decapitated in a Cologne prison. In the end his executioners opted for a *Fallbeil*. It's a sort of guillotine with a blade as sharp as a razor fitted into two runners. His last words were: "I only hope I'll have time to hear the blood spurt from my body." I keep wondering whether his head actually heard anything from inside the basket it rolled into. Rosie tells me about the film, *M*, which she's been to see. It reminded her of *The Three-penny Opera* with all those good-for-nothings living their own lives outside the law, and thinking their community of crooks better than the bourgeoisie. I don't want to listen. I look out of the window and see the curtain move opposite. Tomorrow we're going on vacation to our friends the Siegels on the lakes. I'll be reunited with their daughter, my dear friend Beate.

■ ■ ■

We go boating every day with my father or Beate's, and then she and I catch grasshoppers and keep them in colonies. We also catch butterflies but we release them.

I don't want to go home or back to school. I often tell Mama that all I want is to stay with her and Papa and Beate. She smiles at me, reminds me I love school and tells me about my first day there. I wasn't frightened and I didn't cry, unlike the other children who didn't want to leave their mothers. I wasn't afraid of exploring a new world, I was curious. I remember our teacher, Herr Pichelmann, with his white uniform like my dentist's, and his violin, which he would play to the pupils in his class. Thanks to him, I can read and write. My best friend at school is called Ralph. He's lucky. A chauffeur comes to pick him up from school every day; he climbs into his long black car, as big as our cousins the Bernheimers', and, sitting alone on the backseat, he waves goodbye to me through the window.

I'd like to live here, on the lakes, but I'm also looking forward to seeing Ralph again. Mama has started packing our bags. We'll be going home soon.

The vacation was so long that when we arrived home I'd forgotten Rosie's face. She was waiting for us in the street, by the front door. I didn't recognize her, I thought she was someone else. And yet she was wearing her usual clothes, a long black dress and a white apron. But she'd changed her haircut. It was shorter. She hugged me tight, Papa and Mama shook her hand and we went upstairs. They asked her what had been going on in the city.

"It's getting worse and worse. Demonstrations outside the house every day! In favor of Hitler one day, against him the next. In the morning his supporters come streaming past under his window with their arms raised, and in the evening it's the other side coming through brandishing their fists. Clashes between the demonstrations are more and more violent. They count the dead after each rally. And the rest of the time, there are beggars ringing at the door again and again. With all these elections going on the city's on tenterhooks."

*Not until my fourteenth or fifteenth year did I begin to come across the word "Jew" with any frequency, partly in connection with political discussions. This filled me with a mild distaste, and I could not rid myself of an unpleasant feeling that always came over me whenever religious quarrels occurred in my presence.*

*At that time I did not think anything else of the question.*

—ADOLF HITLER, *MEIN KAMPF*

Rosie's bedroom is next to mine. I sometimes go in to see her in the evening and we sit on her bed. The two of us have a secret: she reads the books from Papa's library and tells me about them. She explains everything, and I remember the things she tells me, stories my parents discuss, thinking I don't understand. Rosie talks to me about politics. She and I are Spartacists. The Spartacists are old-style Communists; they wanted to create a world with no distinctions between rich and poor. Their name comes from the gladiator Spartacus, who freed slaves in Roman times. Rosie confides in me with things she doesn't tell anyone else. She has the same name as her idol Rosa Luxemburg, the leading German Spartacist. Rosie shows me a photo of her idol in a newspaper hidden under her bed. Rosa Luxemburg was against war and against the monarchy, she didn't want the Germans and French to fight, she thought all men were brothers. She would have liked to do away with frontiers, kings, differences. Our emperor Wilhelm II put her in prison for her ideas. He declared war on France, my uncle Berthold fought, and Rosie's fiancé died. When Rosa Luxemburg came out of prison she led a revolution and forced the emperor to step down, and the fighting stopped at last. That was the best day of Rosie's life. But later, friends of the emperor, military men, assassinated Rosa Luxemburg in the hope of resuming the fight. Since then, Rosie's stopped telling people she's a Spartacist. Except me. I wish I were Spartacus the gladiator and I could lead an army of slaves to defeat anyone who wants war.

■ ■ ■

Last week crowds of demonstrators poured past our house. Rosie and I watched them from up in my bedroom. Waves of Nazis flowed between our house and Hitler's. They kept coming all day long. Hitler's SA marched in nice straight lines, like a real army, all wearing red armbands with a white circle and a swastika in the center. They held their arms outstretched toward their leader's room, calling his name, bellowing *"Heil Hitler! Heil Hitler!"* and the windows reverberated like drums to this endless roar. Aunt Bobbie and the duke came down to watch, and we all huddled together behind that fragile window.

"They're savages," Aunt Bobbie said.

"Idiots," the duke added.

"They're so young. Look, they're not even fifteen," Aunt Bobbie whispered. "As if shouting in the streets is all you need do to solve our problems! Verdun wasn't enough for them. They want to fight too, to end up like their fathers and uncles. The glory of killing or being killed. And this hatred of Jews, it's monstrous!"

1932

"Vulgar," said the duke, adjusting his monocle. "Your daughter should talk some sense into her man, my dear."

"But she loves him! And you know she doesn't understand anything about politics. Neither does he, for that matter. I think he only mingles with the Nazis for business."

"For business?"

"Yes, if Hitler ever comes to power, we'd still have to keep the factories going. They say he's preparing to launch major military commands."

"Heaven preserve us."

■ ■ ■

Rosie's more cheerful. Since this morning we've been watching a different crowd processing along our street. It's flowing like a river, like wavelets before the prow of a boat. They're Rosie's friends this time. She's proud, convinced that these men and women will avert another war in Europe. There seem to me to be so many of them, and they look untidy, they don't know how to march in step. Their uniforms are mismatched, dyed different shades of green. They turn at the end of the street, stop outside Hitler's house and thrust their fists toward the sky.


Rosie's been reading the newspaper to me this evening. Her eyes are all red. She's been crying. Papa is pacing back and forth between the drawing room window and the front door. He stops by the papers spread out on the desk, and says to my mother:

"Old Hindenburg has beaten Hitler, yes, but with only fifty-three percent of the vote! Can you imagine? And now the Nazis have two hundred and thirty seats in the Reichstag. They've become the largest force in the country. There are six million unemployed in the streets: that's one in three. Hindenburg will have to appoint him as chancellor. How else can he govern? And to think he secured German nationality only this year! And everyone's joining him: Fritz Thyssen's introduced him to the most powerful industrialists in Düsseldorf. He's told them that democracy is what's causing the crisis, and they believe him! And meanwhile the damnable SA are assassinating people. They killed another sixteen poor boys in the streets of Hamburg on July 17. Hitler has the nerve to ask for mercy for the murderers who are facing the death penalty. Apparently Hjalmar Schacht, the former president of the Reichsbank, is going to support him. Everyone will think the Nazis have credible economic solutions. As if cutting us off from the world, closing the borders and planning for war could make the world a better place."

"Schacht? But we know him!" Mama exclaims.

She looks through the album for a group photograph: my parents posing with other people outside a large building. The picture was taken in Switzerland, in Zurich, at a congress to which Schacht and my father were both invited. Papa is up on the right-hand side, Hjalmar Schacht in the middle, my mother toward the bottom on the left, with the wives.

*1932*

■ ■ ■

Every time we walk past the opera house my mother promises to take me to see something. And today we're here to see *William Tell*, a matinee performance. That's what they call the Sunday performances for children. It's actually the afternoon and there are hardly any children.

I've never seen such a beautiful place. The walls, seats and floor are in red velvet with gold trimmings. The two of us are like a courting couple. I'm wearing a man's suit, a white shirt, a tie and black leather shoes. Sadly my flannel knickerbockers are making my calves itch. Mama is wearing a beautiful green dress that I chose for her. There are war widows dressed in black and lots of invalids wounded in the trenches. One of them has no legs. I noticed in the intermission when the whole audience stood up, except him. His upper half was just like everyone else, with a face like an actor, a very thin mustache and hair greased back over his head, but below his tummy there was nothing. In the bar there was a man with a hook instead of a hand, and when we came back to sit down, a man with a leather nose held the door to the circle open for me. Then the performers took up the story again. I recognize some passages that Mama has played on the piano, then I fall asleep, lulled by the music.

On the way home I tell Mama how much I like my life; I list all the people I love, not forgetting Arabella, whom we haven't seen for a long time. She promises we'll invite her to the house soon.

■ ■ ■

All my parents talk about at home now is Hitler. In the evenings they tell each other what they've learned from their friends during the day. My father has a friend who knows Hitler, Carl Schmitt, a serious writer who is sometimes a guest in our house. Between these visits, Carl Schmitt and Papa write to each other. Papa reads out his letters to us over breakfast. They're all about politics, and Germany. I find them boring.

This evening my father and the duke are discussing the news. I listen in silence.

"This Schleicher isn't such a bad chancellor," says my father. "Hindenburg was shrewd to choose him for the job. The Nazis are backing off. Now that they're in Parliament, people can see they don't have a magic wand. They lost two million votes in the November 6 elections. Schleicher is pitting Hitler against his rival, Otto Strasser, and they're tearing each other apart. Apparently our neighbor's on the brink of suicide."

"In the meantime his forces are keeping up their vile work," the duke cautions. "There were more than a hundred thousand children, all in uniform, chanting Hitler's name at the Hitler Youth National Congress in Potsdam on October first. Ernst Röhm's SA prowl our cities by night. There's talk of over two hundred political assassinations in the streets. Old Hindenburg hosts Hitler in his own home. That old fighter pilot, Hermann Göring, also rubs shoulders with him. To think he appointed that brute as president of the Reichstag. As for their friend Joseph Goebbels, the treacherous little runt, the so-called intellectual who runs their pestilential newspaper, *Der Angriff*. Do you know what he said? 'We're infiltrating the Reichstag like wolves in a sheepfold.' Hardly reassuring, I must say!"

"It's 1932, for goodness' sake!" my father retorts. "People are informed. No one wants a dictatorship. No, I'm not worried."

My mother has made me promise to stop telling people we're Jewish. When I go to Rosie's bedroom in the evenings, she keeps telling me the Jews aren't a race but the people who practice a particular religion, and anyway we don't have to take up the same religion as our parents, or have a faith at all. We're born free to believe in God or not, and therefore to be Jewish or not. She explains that the Jews have been bullied for centuries, they were denied the right to own land, but they're humans just like everyone else, and perhaps even more deserving because they've been constantly persecuted. She's getting emotional, telling me I mustn't be ashamed of being a Jew and citing the names of Jews who've achieved great things. She tells me about Karl Marx, whom she greatly admires, and recounts his whole life for me, and then Rosa Luxemburg's—she was also a Jew.

"Hitler's talking garbage. He says the Jews are all Communists, and then the next minute he claims they run the banks—but most of the banks in Germany are managed by Protestants! He says the Jews don't want to share anything, when the man who campaigned most vigorously for spreading wealth around was Karl Marx—a professed Jew. As for Leon Trotsky, he was born into a Jewish family. Hitler criticizes them for other things too, of course. He claims the Communist revolution is a Jewish conspiracy! Even though Stalin, the leader of the USSR, isn't Jewish, any more than other Communist leaders around the world are, Ernst Thälmann in Germany, Maurice Thorez in France. And what about Albert Einstein, the greatest scientist of all time, and born in Germany, should we hate him because his parents grew up in the Jewish faith? And Sigmund Freud too, perhaps? You remember, I told you about him, he's the man who heals people with words; he's learning to understand dreams, and he says we keep all our memories inside us, even those we think we've forgotten. Hitler wants to ban books by these great men, to turn his back on their discoveries; he's superstitious, illiterate and obsessed with dark forces that don't exist. He's like the barbarians who thought there were ogres in the woods and who loved warfare and sacking villages. He's less sophisticated than the Greeks three thousand years back. You just remember, my little Bürschi, you must never be ashamed of who you are."

Rosie's bought a copy of *Mein Kampf*, and she shows it to me. It's the book Hitler wrote, the book about his life. She's underlined passages all the way through.

"I've never read anything as contemptible as this book, my little Bürschi. But don't worry about it. We Spartacists will make sure he eats the dust."

I cuddle up close to her and she kisses my forehead.

■ ■ ■

Today's the first day of term at Gebeleschule, my new school. I'm worried I won't know anyone and won't have any friends. Luckily, Mama's promised that Ralph will be there too. The birds woke me early this morning. Rosie had laid my clothes out ready yesterday, folded on the dresser. By the feet of the wicker chair I spot my new satchel, just like my father's, but smaller. So shiny it reflects the light of the breaking dawn. I look out of the window. In the street, a guard is smoking a cigarette next to Hitler's Mercedes. I'd never noticed it has a headlight in the middle of the radiator grille, like the eye of the Cyclops in the adventures of Ulysses. Rosie says that Hitler cowrote his book with his driver, proof that it's a bad book. Is it the same man smoking outside my house now?

I hear noise from the kitchen, where my hot chocolate is being prepared. The smell of toast seeps under the door and I follow it all the way to Rosie.

Mama walks me to Gebeleschule. Children wait outside the gates, accompanied by their mothers or nannies. Ralph is there with his mother. She's wearing a green dress, high heels, and a maroon hat that matches her dark red lips. She takes off a glove and shakes Mama's hand. Ralph and I leave them. We have to join the others in our group, standing in straight lines in front of a door at the far end of the schoolyard. We're lucky, we're in the same class. I keep a firm grip on the handle of my leather satchel.

Our teacher is called Fräulein Weikl. She's full of enthusiasm, all smiles as she flits from desk to desk, writes on the blackboard, rubs it out, writes some more. She's pretty, her hair is even blonder than Ralph's, almost white. Her eyes are so blue they seem to be lit from the inside. She's much younger than my mother, almost like a big sister. Ralph doesn't sit next to me but we meet up at break time, and we leave together at the end of the day. Rosie's there with my snack, she kisses Ralph and we watch him leave in the back of his English car, a Rolls-Royce.

■ ■ ■

It's Ralph's birthday party this afternoon. We received the invitation in the mail. It said that afternoon tea would start at three o'clock and go on till six. At three o'clock precisely Rosie and I are outside the gate to the villa, a big green gate on the street. We go in and our footsteps crunch loudly on the gravel. The villa is set in a large flower-filled garden, and tall chestnut trees hide the upstairs windows. On the lawn stands a table covered with a white tablecloth, and there tartlets, cakes and fruit juices wait patiently. Children I've never met before are running around the garden. I'm still holding Rosie's hand. We climb a staircase up to the house and step inside. Feeling intimidated, I keep my eyes on the hall floor: a checkerboard of black and white. The drawing room door stands open, and a woman with her back to us is playing Mozart on a grand piano, a minuet that I can play faultlessly. At the far end of the room, an old harp snoozes beside a tapestry hanging that Ralph has described to me: Narcissus admiring his reflection in the water just before he drowns, the nymph Echo on the edge of the woods trying to hold him back. The drawing room reminds me of Frederick the Great's, the one that was reconstructed in *The Flute Concert of Sans-Souci*. At the end of the film, Frederick's friend was executed on his father's orders. My sister, Dorle, loved it, she said the actress, Renate Müller, was as beautiful as Marlene Dietrich.

Ralph has appeared. He wants to shake Rosie's hand, but she kisses him as usual. He takes me by the shoulder and leads me off to introduce me to his parents. They're sitting at the end of the drawing room, along with his grandparents—an old man who looks like Marshal von Hindenburg, and a woman as small and wizened as a mummy. First his mother greets me with a smile, extending her hand to me and addressing me formally as if talking to an adult. Standing beside her is Ralph's father.

1932

He was a pilot in the war and Ralph has promised he'll tell me about his adventures.

"Ralph, do introduce us to your little friend…And what is your name, sir?"

"Edgar…"

"Show your little friend how people greet me here."

Ralph deposits a kiss on the end of his father's nose. I imitate him; his father's nose is cold.

"Could you tell us about your dogfights, Papa? I promised Edgar you would."

And his father tells us all sorts of stories, how he perfected his first plane himself, and took off from a field below their castle in the country. He describes air battles, and how he worked out a way to detect enemy planes when they were hidden higher up in the clouds, against the sun. He would take a turkey with him and it would gobble when an enemy plane approached. Ralph's father was caught and imprisoned. He was well treated by the French officers and met up with a childhood friend, Robert de B., who invited him to his mess in the evenings. While there, he gained weight and improved his French! He tells us about France and its food, describing its succulent desserts with their strange names: choux pastry treats named after lightning bolts, cream puffs named after nuns, and even a chocolate-coated delicacy called a "negro in a shirt"! He still frequently visits France on business. He tells us about the streets of Paris, the Eiffel Tower, Notre-Dame Cathedral, and the Louvre Museum, and promises to take us one day. We'll travel in a sleeping car or in the zeppelin. He asks me what my father does.

When I tell him he's an editor, and that my uncle Lion is a writer, I can tell he knows them. But he doesn't comment further, and asks me whether I like reading. I say I love books, and he tells Ralph he should follow my example. He talks about various French authors. His favorite is Marcel Proust, who was a childhood friend of his. I recognize the name. My father's often talked about him, and of Walter Benjamin. I ask Ralph's father whether there's a connection between the two writers.

"Aha! Herr Edgar's a connoisseur. In fact, that's almost right. They never met because Proust died shortly before the war. But Walter Benjamin has just translated his novel, with Franz Hessel, unless I'm mistaken. You should take an interest in literature, Ralph."

I've flushed scarlet. And Ralph is a little embarrassed too. So I claim that Ralph is better at reading than me.

■ ■ ■

We don't have school today, and Rosie's taking me to the movies in a huge theater with red velvet seats: we're going to see *Mädchen in Uniform*—a talkie! The lights have gone out, music fills the auditorium and the screen lights up. The film is set in a girls' boarding school in Prussia, and the girls are the same age as Dorle. It's a strange story, it makes my head spin. In the middle of the school there's a staircase as tall as a building. Each floor is open to the staircase. The girls talk to each other from one story to the next, over the void. The heroine drinks alcohol, tells her schoolmistress she loves her, then wants to kill herself and climbs over the banister rail. She passes out and loses her grip, but she's held back before she falls. The girls are disruptive, ganging up together and resisting their overly strict teachers.

As we leave the theater I say that tomorrow I'll ask Ralph if he wants to gang up with me, like in the film. Right now, we're meeting my father at the Fürstenhof Café on Kaunfingerstrasse. We find him on the first floor in a cloud of acrid smoke and a hubbub of male voices. He comes here every day for a cup of coffee topped with whipped cream, and to read the foreign papers. He translates the papers spread out before him for me: The *Corriere della Sera* from Italy, *Le Temps* from Switzerland and *The Times* from England. The pages are big, held on wooden poles, and on them are pictures of the crowds that flocked past our house the other day. There are also pictures of Hitler and other figures I recognize: Joseph Stalin and Hirohito, the emperor of Japan, as well as Mussolini. Rosie's talked to me about him, and I say his name out loud when I see the picture.

"You must always remember these photographs, Bürschi," Papa tells me.

■ ■ ■

I feel quite grown-up, I'm nine already. Next year I'll be able to walk to school all on my own. I meet up with Ralph every day and we talk about everything. This morning I told him about the film. We sealed a pact: whatever happens in life, we'll always be friends. I told him my secret about Rosie and me, and he swore never to tell anyone. He wants to be a Spartacist too. Along with other friends, we played rebelling slaves all day. Then the teacher asked me to stand at the front to recite a poem by Goethe, it's the centenary of his death this year. I'd learned the poem carefully with Rosie: it's the story of a boy, an apprentice sorcerer, whose master goes out. In his absence, the boy does something he's never been allowed to do: he uses his powers and brings to life inanimate objects in the kitchen, but they soon ignore his orders and break everything in sight. To stop them, he decides to smash them up with an axe, which reminds me of the *Fallbeil* used on the Vampire of Düsseldorf, and of Frederick II, who was executed with an axe in *The Flute Concert of Sans-Souci*. As I recited the poem, I thought about the words I was saying, and I saw images. The verse reminded me of the Thomas Mann book on Papa's desk, *Mario and the Magician*. Rosie's told me about it, explaining that the magician, a hypnotist, is actually the dictator Benito Mussolini. Rosie said Hitler's "a great master of hypnosis" like him.

My teacher said, "Well done," and I realized I was miles away. That happens a lot. When I went back to my desk I noticed Ralph was staring at me. Later we were playing in a corner of the yard, and I told him the story of *Mario the Magician*, and how it was really about Benito Mussolini and Adolf Hitler. I said that at home everyone keeps talking about the elections this Sunday. Ralph said it's the same at his house, and there's also a lot of talk about Hitler. Then he asked me what it feels like being Jewish.

*1932*

"It doesn't feel like anything…until someone talks about it. Then it makes me slightly ashamed. I know I shouldn't be embarrassed, because it's just a religion like any other. And I don't yet know if I'm a Jew, anyway. I love Jesus. Even though I'm not completely sure I believe in God, or rather, that I've chosen the god I like best: in Greek times there were dozens of gods. At the end of the day, I'd rather be a Spartacist! With no god or master!"

"Me too. Hooray for Spartacists! Hooray for the slaves' revolt!"

And then Ralph told me his secret. His parents are going to vote for Adolf Hitler.

*Notwithstanding that Vienna in those days counted nearly two hundred thousand Jews among its two million inhabitants, I did not see them. In the first few weeks my eyes and my senses were not equal to the flood of values and ideas. Not until calm gradually returned and the agitated picture began to clear did I look around me more carefully in my new world, and then among other things I encountered the Jewish question.*

—ADOLF HITLER, *MEIN KAMPF*, ON HIS EARLY YEARS IN VIENNA

We were at home. Mama was playing a piece by Handel, humming along in time as her fingers worked the keyboard. It was *Sarabande*, slow, drawn-out music. Next she played a piece that Elly Ney had performed at a concert Mama took me to. Elly Ney is a pianist, she's one of the most famous in the world. I must have been the youngest spectator in the concert hall, and yet I knew every piece she played: Mozart's *Turkish March*, Beethoven's *Moonlight* Sonata...

Mama moved aside so I could sit at the piano and play. I chose a movement by Handel, *Passacaglia*, a piece that gets louder, then softer and then faster and faster. Mama told me I'll be a great pianist one day, like Edwin Fischer, whom we'd heard performing the day before. As she stroked my hair and the back of my neck, the door opened.

"Hitler's been appointed chancellor," Papa announced.

I stopped playing for a moment, but then resumed the piece, with one ear on their conversation. Rosie came over and Aunt Bobbie came downstairs with the duke. They were all silent. I started to play the *Passacaglia* again. Papa said he'd just spoken on the telephone with Uncle Lion, who was traveling abroad: an ambassador had advised him not to return to Germany for now. Papa asked me to go to my room because it was late. I sat at the end of my bed working on my model of a Märklin, a fighter plane that now stands on the dresser in my room.

In the last two days things have been happening quickly in Berlin, where my sister lives. I read about it in the *Münchner Neueste Nachrichten*, edited by an acquaintance of my father's. Mama and Papa talk about it all the time and have given up trying to stop me listening.

"Hindenburg's let him make Göring his minister for home affairs, you know the one," Papa says, "that irascible aviator. An hour later he banned demonstrations, and insisted on monitoring every publication in the country. It's beyond comprehension. It's as if we were at war again. The old marshal has agreed that that madman Röhm's wretched SA—that gang of thugs dressed up as soldiers—should be auxiliaries to the police force. Bandits responsible for enforcing order, what next! And why? I just can't believe it! And do you know how many of them there are? Three million. And fifty thousand of them are now considered actual policemen. The same men who assassinated more than a hundred people last year!"

"But, darling, don't you think all this excess is down to Hitler's entourage?" my mother asks. "It's bound to calm down, isn't it? Once they've had a chance to swagger about in the streets, they really will have to run the country, as others have before them. They'll be confronted with the same problems. You can't solve everything with a cudgel! And it will all go back to normal. Don't you think now that Hitler's been appointed he'll toe the line? He'll certainly have to follow the regulations set by the League of Nations. The other countries won't let him flout the agreements reached after the war without doing something. He knows that…Hitler can't be as out of control as people say."

"But of course he is!" my father says heatedly. "His friends are dangerous, ill-educated lunatics. But Hitler's the worst of the lot. I took the trouble to read his doorstop from cover to cover. And, as Sigmund Freud said, what we're seeing are the harebrained schemes of a hysteric. He's a paranoiac and thinks he's found a magic formula for ruling the world. He has a preposterous explanation for everything, and he thinks his arguments are infallibly logical. He sets them out over pages and pages, he wants to indoctrinate us with his own meandering, tortuous thought processes, and there's nothing rational about any

1933

of it, I can tell you. It's terrifying. It really is the work of a deranged mind, a megalomaniac. In fact, it's so crazy that I can't help laughing when I read it."

"Perhaps we should leave Germany, then?" my mother asks tentatively.

"Leave? That would certainly make the Nazis happy. But where would we go? Who would have us? We'd need a work visa for whichever country we choose. We really can't settle illegally wherever takes our fancy. With this financial crash, foreigners everywhere are being accused of taking other people's jobs, illegal immigrants are being driven out to limit the rise of the extreme right. We'd be foreigners with no papers, like all those people who've already fled Mussolini's Italy, or the civil war in Spain. The republicans are fighting in the streets with the Fascists. Civil war...that's the worst thing...It would cost us a fortune to leave like that, we'd lose everything, and with no work our savings would melt away in a matter of weeks. And what would we live off? And Bürschi's only just started school, where would he go to school? In France? Or England? He doesn't speak a word of French or English...Imagine him waiting months in some camp. Can you picture us, stateless, behind barbed wire, waiting endlessly for someone to rubber-stamp our papers?"

"America?" my mother suggests.

"But it's such a long way away! And anyway they're very careful about giving out visas. And over there, it would be impossible to make anyone believe you're there for a vacation and then stay forever. They're draconian when you board the ship and when you arrive. It's very hard."

"Palestine? Lots of Jews go there to make their home..."

"But it's a desert, my darling," Papa says gently. "People live on the sand, like the Bedouin. And what will the Arabs say when they find out that Germans have moved onto their land because they weren't wanted in their own country? The anti-Semites are at work in Palestine too! Anyway, it's too hot in summer and too cold in winter. I'd have to work the land, you'd have to run a farm, feed hens. You could say goodbye to your beautiful gowns, to playing the piano and concerts. And there's nothing to say the Jews will ever secure independence from that British protectorate. Even if they do, I wonder how long they'd keep it. In the desert, men are still just as ready to fight so they can plant their flag on their neighbor's plot of land."

"But, I don't know, there must be *something* we can do..."

"If it were just the two of us, on our own, yes. But we're a family. I've contemplated every option: Switzerland, Czechoslovakia, the Netherlands, everything. Whichever country you name, it's more than we can afford. Nations are going under one after the other: Italy, Japan, and now Spain. There are more and more Fascists everywhere, in France, the United States..."

"It's worst here," Mama says. "They say the Nazis are planning to build camps to intern anyone who opposes their ideas."

"They don't mean the Jews, just the Communists. The camps are for political opponents. Don't worry. We just have to wait till the next elections. People will soon have enough of being steamrollered. Everyone wants peace. We all like to read the papers, travel, go for walks. They're already saying that the Nazis won't have a majority in the parliamentary elections on March fifth. They'll be in free fall!"

I play in my bedroom. The lights are always out in Hitler's house these days. Since he became chancellor, there are round-the-clock guards outside the building. I've played with my Christmas presents, and I'm lying alone in bed, reading stories by Karl May, an explorer who traveled in Saudi Arabia and Yemen. I'd like to go to a faraway country. Why does my father say we wouldn't be happy? I'd cross the desert on a camel, single file in a long caravan, from oasis to palm grove. I'd see mirages and sand castles. I dream I'm dressed like a Bedouin, I have my own curved dagger, and I'm galloping on a purebred Arabian. I dream of sleeping under the stars on an endless sand dune.

■ ■ ■

Hitler has been chancellor for three weeks and the elections are in five days. They're going to vote to elect the new congressmen in the Reichstag. Uncle Lion has decided to wait for the results before returning to Germany. Everyone says the Nazis will lose.

In this morning's *Münchner Neueste Nachrichten* there are pictures of burning buildings. It's the Reichstag itself.

"Thank goodness he's not a Jew," Papa says.

"Why do you say that?" Mama asks.

"Haven't you heard? Have you not read the articles? It's all anyone can talk about. They've arrested the man who started the fire, Marinus van der Lubbe, a Dutch Communist of just twenty-four. Only a day has passed and Hitler is revoking many of our liberal laws. In the name of protecting democracy, of course. He claims Germany is under threat from terrorists, the Communists and foreigners. According to him, this fire was the signal for the launch of some huge insurrection. That very day Hindenburg signed a presidential decree 'for the protection of the people and the country.' Shall I read you the article? It's a summary: 'Article one suspends most of the civil liberties guaranteed by the Weimar Republic— freedom of the individual, freedom of expression, freedom of the press, the right to form societies and to have public meetings, confidentiality of mail and telephone services, protection of the home and property. Articles two and three transfer various prerogatives usually reserved for the *Länder* to the Reich government. Articles four and five institute heavy penalties for particular crimes, principally the death penalty for arson in public buildings. And article six sets out that the decree takes effect from the day of its proclamation.'"

"But surely they can't do that without Parliament's approval?" Mama asks, still calm.

"Hitler made a speech to the congressmen. Obviously no one wanted to be seen to be siding with terrorists and enemies of democracy. The whole assembly rose to their feet when he sang the national anthem. He's Machiavellian. And simplistic: in his view, opposing his ideas is tantamount to supporting terrorism. He keeps bandying about the danger of a Bolshevik revolution. It's unanswerable. The net result is that his henchmen are already making multiple arrests among the Communists. Friends have called me. Even Ernst Thälmann has fled!"

"The Communist leader? But six million Germans have just voted for him..."

"He'll be arrested," Papa says matter-of-factly. "I can guarantee that if this Marinus were a Jew, every synagogue in the country would already be ablaze."

"What next?"

"What's next is the end of the Weimar Republic, the end of the republic, period."


I don't want to listen to the adults anymore, they're boring. Ralph says it's the same at his house. He doesn't want to hear any more either. Together we play at inventing a world with no wars or borders. When the kids in the schoolyard have play fights, we move away. We sit side by side reading Karl May. One day we'll set off on a voyage together, without telling our parents. They'll be impressed and proud when we return famous, followed by a retinue of servants laden with exotic gifts...But when I come home, the mood is glum. Before, Papa used to play with me, he'd go down on all fours, I'd climb on his back, then he'd roll me over and tickle me. But he doesn't feel like it now. He gets angry so quickly. My mother looks tired, she says life is difficult.

I watch them in secret, hiding behind my bedroom door. I can see them through the gap. They're talking about Thomas Mann.

"He's with Lion, in France," Papa tells Mama.

"In the South, at Sanary?"

"Yes. The Nazis have been to Lion's house. They've ransacked the place, broken the windows, knocked over the bookshelves, like the Huns. The house is ruined. All the poetry of that carefully created haven gone just like that. They've done the same to Thomas Mann's house."

"Good God!" Mama exclaims. "But why Thomas Mann? He's neither a Jew nor Communist…"

"No, but he's 'decadent,' almost as serious an offense as being 'degenerate,' which is what those madmen say we are."

■ ■ ■

I don't like it when my parents go out in the evening, I'm afraid they won't come back, that they'll be arrested and sent to a camp. Rosie told me that the Communist Party leader Ernst Thälmann has been arrested, along with lots of his friends. They've been penned up in shacks at Dachau, not far from Munich.

■ ■ ■

Rosie came to pick me up at school, as she does every day. She had a snack in her basket. It was a nice day so we went to eat it in the park. I was allowed to spend some time on the swings. Soldiers marched past in small groups, all wearing armbands with swastikas. Their feet made a rhythmic sound, like drumbeats, or hammer blows on an anvil. I could hear the gravel crunch under their boots. Rosie turned away whenever one of them looked toward us. She was silent on the way home. Mama was at home but she didn't make me do my homework, she asked Rosie to look after me. I didn't get my usual hug, and now I'm in bed. I would have liked to play for a while after dinner but wasn't allowed to. I don't know what's going on today, everything's different. Cars go by outside in the street. Doors slam. I can hear Papa and Mama talking in the drawing room.

"They've put a giant swastika on the front of the town hall," Papa's saying. "He's been chancellor for barely a month, and he already has the temerity to decorate the city in his party's colors. I don't understand. It's completely illegal. But that's not the worst of it. The SS* are now in charge of Munich's police force. Hitler has ordered that all power should be handed over to Himmler, his head of security. They've announced officially that this new police force is declaring war on Communists, Marxists…and Jews. They've made some arrests today. Packs of them are bursting into shops, breaking everything,

---

* *Schutzstaffel*, which means "protection squad."

and frog-marching the owners and their employees out. We're living a nightmare."

■ ■ ■

The atmosphere is gloomy again today. Mama didn't want to help me with my homework. She handed me over to Rosie. We're in the kitchen now for teatime but I've had enough of not being with Mama. I want to sit on her lap and play the piano. In the next room my parents are talking about the father of Beate Siegel; she and I used to hunt for butterflies and grasshoppers beside the lake in summer.

*1933*

"...it's one of his clients, Herr Uhlfelder," I hear Papa say. "The Nazis destroyed his shop yesterday, just after they took over control of the police force, and they arrested him. No one knows where he is. Michael went to the police station this morning to have him released. Since then there's been no news of *him* either."

I have my nose practically inside my bowl of hot chocolate, I can hear my own breathing. I sit here watching the changing colors in the milk, not wanting to eat the skin. I'm glad my parents are safe at home. Beate's father could be killed. Rosie sits in silence.

I do my homework, take my bath, have my supper. I read a story in bed. It's still daylight outside. The telephone's been ringing all evening. I can hear Papa's voice from the drawing room. I know he's talking about Beate's father, Herr Siegel.

"…and then a detachment of SA took Michael into a small office. They beat him ruthlessly and broke two of his teeth. They tore his pants, then put a sign around his neck with the words: 'I'm a Jew and I'll never criticize the police again,' and they made him go out into the street. They forced him to walk barefoot through Munich all day, trailing him around, like a slave, a fairground animal, a curiosity. People stood and stared. Then they put the barrel of a rifle to his temple and, without any explanation, laughed and said he was free to go. He managed to take a taxi and get home. He's in bed. Alive."

■ ■ ■

Mama's brother has mailed us a French magazine, *L'Illustration*. The cover has a photograph of English children in the streets. They seem to be playing hopscotch. English words are daubed on the ground in white paint: "Boycott German Goods. Open Palestine." Papa translates for me as usual.

He shows me the whole magazine. There are photos of soldiers, the Reichswehr armed forces marching on the parade square of the Lustgarten royal palace in Berlin. The text says that "batteries fired salutes in front of the cathedral." I look at the pictures of cannons mounted on trucks.

"It's the end of the republic, Bürschi. Take a really good look, you mustn't forget this."

The next page features a large photo of the inside of the church in Potsdam. He reads a sentence out loud:

" 'This marks the fall of the Weimar Republic and the accession of the Third Reich.' "

I can see Hitler, teeny tiny, standing at a lectern. I recognize him. I also make out Marshal von Hindenburg sitting in front of him.

Papa reads the caption, " 'The opening ceremony of the new Reichstag in the garrison church in Potsdam on March 21. On the right, VIP boxes; at the back, Hitler's congressmen in their black shirts; in the foreground, representatives of the Catholic Center and local politicians; in the central enclosure reserved for members of the government, Chancellor Hitler reading his speech before President von Hindenburg in his marshal's uniform.' "

On the left-hand page, a smaller photograph shows soldiers with Nazi armbands saluting each other.

"Look, they're outside the main doors to the Kroll Opera House in Berlin, where the provisional Parliament has been set up. That picture was taken two days after this one, two weeks ago."

And he reads the article to Mama. I don't catch everything, but I listen. I like the way his voice changes when he reads, soft and quiet.

" 'Breaking with tradition, it was not the eldest statesman but President Göring who pronounced the speeches open. In the absence of any opposition, proceedings were extremely orderly and the election took place without incident. It was in this same enclosure that, on March 23, the chancellor read out his declaration of government. This long document does not feature the party leader's usual robust language. All these parliamentary demonstrations

*1933*

were effectively intended solely to secure a proposed law conferring full power to the government. This proposal delegates to the executive every prerogative that has hitherto been covered by the legislature: the right to legislate even on budgetary matters, the right to alter the Constitution; the normal relationship between the president of the empire and Parliament is suspended, and the chancellor will now be promulgating laws. The president's role in the Reichstag will be reduced to ratifying bills. This exceptional regime is intended to last for a four-year period, until April 1, 1937. The election was won by four hundred and forty-one votes to ninety-four, out of five hundred and thirty-five congressmen, with the eighty-three Communists banned from the Assembly and some dozen Socialists currently in prison. The Reichstag then adjourned sine die. Chancellor Hitler, therefore, now has unrestricted dictatorship.'"

Another photograph shows men walking around a large courtyard.

"German political prisoners taking exercise outside Berlin's administrative buildings," Papa reads.

"Doesn't it say anything about Jews?" Mama asks.

"Yes, it does: 'The anti-Semitic campaign has also been implemented so aggressively that many Jews, particularly in intellectual circles, have felt they had to leave Germany. Around the world, most notably in the United States and England, their coreligionists have taken the initiative of setting up a protest movement, which is likely to have far-reaching scope.'"

"Is that all?"

"That's all."

Mama looks disappointed. She picks up the paper and turns over the pages as if looking for something. Her eyes are red. She puts down the paper and goes to her bedroom.

■ ■ ■

Since Hitler's been running Germany, Fräulein Weikl at school has changed, she talks about him a lot. We've started work in a new exercise book this week. She'll be asking us to draw in it every day. I like coloring my drawings. I have a pencil box with color crayons, a lead pencil and a fountain pen. I put my ink pot in a small hole in the corner of my desk. I want to start straightaway!

"This exercise book is like the beginning of a new life for us and for Germany," says Fräulein Weikl.

■ ■ ■

It's May 1 today, International Workers' Day. Rosie meets up with her friends on this date every year. They go off with provisions under their arms and join parades in the streets, then they dance and have fun in the evening. Bands play cheerful tunes, paper lanterns light up the city's squares where tables and benches have been set up for the festivities.

For the first time, the date wasn't observed today: Hitler replaced it with a different occasion, celebrating his party. Fräulein Weikl told us that from now on it would be a day "for real workers, the ones who love their country, not the lazy ones who never want to do anything." And she suggested we each do a drawing on the subject. I took my new exercise book from my satchel, opened it out nice and flat and took my inspiration from the picture my teacher had drawn on the blackboard. First, I very carefully drew a big hammer, the Communist symbol. On this hammer, I wrote the words "May 1." Then I drew a swastika. Completely covering the hammer. I colored it all with crayons. It's my best drawing ever. I don't want to show it to Rosie, in case it upsets her. It makes it look as if the Nazis have won the war against the Spartacists.

■ ■ ■

We write and draw in our books every day. Fräulein Weikl says I have some of the best handwriting in the class. We write in Gothic script with beautiful joined-up letters, solemn letters. She gives us history and geography lessons. I understand the war better now. I've drawn a magnificent eagle, and a Celtic cross, and I wrote "1914–1918." It looks like a real poster. I've made a map of Germany, not forgetting the regions stolen by other countries. We lost the war but at just four against twenty-seven, it was an unequal fight, our enemies behaved like cowards! We talk about it every day. We've all copied out tables into our exercise books, giving a tally of our family members killed or injured for the fatherland. A solid line for each man injured, a cross for the dead. There were three columns, one for fathers, one for uncles and one for grandfathers. I had one solid line, for my uncle Berthold. I raised my hand and went to the front of the class to describe how he walked for miles and miles, lived in the trenches, fought day and night without sleep, with shells falling close to him, killing his fellow soldiers. I also said that he thought we should have won the war, and Fräulein Weikl straightened her shoulders, puffed out her chest and smiled, her eyes glistening. Her voice quavered as she told me well done. She seemed proud of me, and I was too.

*1933*

I'm really happy at this school. Our teacher's wonderful. She's even more beautiful than Dorle, she's as gentle as my mother and she's always kind to me. I like looking at her. I think she thinks I'm special. When I copy out work, stick in a picture or color a drawing, she comes behind me and watches over my shoulder. I can hear her breathing. I'm aware of her perfume, hanging in the air around me, and I bask in it. She leans over me and takes my hand to show me how to improve my letters. Her palm is soft against my fingers. Her hair is perfumed.

The weather outside is beautiful today and sunbeams warm my cheeks as I work. I've stuck in a photograph of a horse standing alone by a soldier's grave. You can see he's sad because he's lost his master. I used a ruler to draw a black frame around it, as neat as a real picture frame. That soldier could have been my uncle. Will I die in a war?

"Germany had to break up her army after the Great War: at one time we had frigates and triplanes, we were the most powerful…but we were betrayed," our teacher tells us.

I've cut out two photos from the paper and stuck them facing each other, one on each page. The first is of a statue of a soldier. There are flowers strewn at his feet, and military crosses, and banners embroidered with farewell messages from his family and his surviving brothers-in-arms. On the opposite page, edged with lines drawn with a wooden ruler, is an engraving of a cross standing in a huge, bleak field. The grave of a forgotten soldier, lost on that great plain. In the distance are a few isolated trees that look like a line of soldiers. Two mournful pictures facing each other. They're both gray as the sky on a rainy day. When Fräulein Weikl sees me looking at them, she strokes my hair.

"Every week," she tells us, "German workers load hundreds of train wagons with corn, coal and other supplies even though we're very short of them ourselves. These trains are sent to France to feed our enemies, who are terribly rich as it is. German politicians had to agree to these privations in order to end hostilities. The twenty-seven countries that we fought on our own insisted on these unfair conditions. Our soldiers, who'd suffered so much, were about to win their last battles. Meanwhile, tucked away comfortably in cities, far from the front, lazy, greedy, corrupt politicians capitulated to the enemy and stabbed our heroes in the back."

My most impressive drawing is of a swastika above a rising sun. On the opposite page I've stuck a photo of Hitler standing in front of an airplane: a girl older than me is handing him some flowers; beside her is a boy my age, looking straight at him. Hitler seems to be smiling, he's leaning toward the girl, saying something to her. Another girl watches the scene enviously. Behind the children are mothers with the same admiring expression Fräulein Weikl has when the headmaster comes into the classroom and tells us he's pleased with us. The Führer is wearing a swastika armband. Using my crayons, I've done a picture of twenty-five swastikas and a sunrise over the countryside.

I'm happier at school than at home. My parents are short-tempered, they scold me over the tiniest thing and talk about politics the whole time. When friends come to visit, Mama and Papa are pleasant while they're around, then the moment they've left the questions start: Are they real friends? Can we trust them? Ralph and I ask ourselves the same questions at school: Which of our friends can we trust? Some are not as dependable as they seem!

■ ■ ■

Uncle Lion won't ever return to Germany. Hitler has stripped him of his nationality. All his books have been burned. Soldiers went into bookshops, confiscated them, then piled them up in the street, so many of them they looked like hills. The soldiers doused them with gas and set them alight. Still, Uncle Lion seems to be happy in France, he lives in a hotel by the sea with Thomas Mann's family. They've created a mini Germany. Marcel Proust's translator, Franz Hessel, the man Ralph's father mentioned to me, is there with them. Mama wants us to go and join them.

Mama's brother Heinrich, who had to sell his villa on the lake after Black Thursday, has also left Germany. He's in Paris.

■ ■ ■

It's soon to be the vacation! In the schoolyard every morning we stand in rows and have to raise our arms for a long time while we sing the national anthem. Our shoulders get stiff and sore. Ralph has come up with a trick, and we've passed it on to the others: we rest our arms on the shoulders of the boy in front. Of course if Fräulein Weikl comes over, we raise the arm correctly. She doesn't notice a thing and glides past, smiling, patting us amicably for doing so well.

■ ■ ■

Uncle Heinrich lent us his chalet for the vacation. Time accelerates when I'm not at school. Almost before each day had begun it seemed to be over, and I had to go to bed. And that was even though the days were long, with the sun waking me in the mornings and not setting till after I went to bed. I went fishing with my father every day, and my mother served up our catches for dinner. Papa helped me build an enormous den. It had a door made of a latticework of leaves and branches, and a roof covered with foliage, which made a rat-a-tat-tat sound on rainy days. I invited my parents in for tea one time. I gave them sweetened lemon juice—I'd squeezed the lemons myself. We carved our initials in the bark of a tree using flints, like in prehistoric times.

■ ■ ■

We're back home now. I was happy to see my friends again and we compared our suntans in the schoolyard. I was whitest of all. Ralph has very dark skin. He's blond but never gets sunburn. Fräulein Weikl asked us to take turns telling the class what we did during the vacation. I stood in front of the blackboard and explained how you attach an earthworm to a fishing hook, and how to make a cork float. I described the gudgeons we caught in the lake; I drew a sketch to show how to catch the wind in a sail, trim a jib and hike when the boat's heeling. But I didn't tell the secret story. I think of it often. I've told that only to Ralph, and made him swear not to tell anyone.

We were having lunch when someone knocked at the door to the chalet. Papa opened up and two soldiers came in. It was the Gestapo. I was frightened they'd arrest us. They asked for our papers, and Mama went to fetch them. Then they asked where the other documents were hidden, my uncle Heinrich's papers. My parents looked at each other in amazement. The soldiers barged past us and started searching. They inspected every room in the house. They turned over mattresses, emptied canisters of peas, rice and pasta, even jam jars. They rummaged through drawers and wardrobes. They unfolded clothes, turning jacket sleeves and pant legs inside out. They quizzed Mama about her brother, Uncle Heinrich. Mama said she knew nothing, that he'd left without giving an address, but had simply said she could use his house while he was away. It went on all afternoon. When half a sandwich fell butter-side-down on the floor, I put it back on the plate without a word. The soldiers didn't notice anything, eating their sandwiches in silence, and I was proud of the trick I'd played. Then the nastier of the two turned to the other man and said out loud, "These Yids don't have anything here. Let's go."

They left, my parents didn't utter a word of comment, and we ate lunch in silence.

The sun was setting already.

■ ■ ■

During break we formed a very tight circle around Thomas, who's top of the class. He lives next door to Hitler's personal photographer, Heinrich Hoffmann. I know the house because I sometimes walk home with Thomas. One time we saw the photographer drive out of his underground garage in his gray Mercedes, a beautiful machine as streamlined as a racing car. So there we all were standing around Thomas in the schoolyard and he told us he'd seen Hitler on Sunday. I said I often saw Hitler because he lives opposite me, and Thomas yelled that he'd seen him closer up than me: Hitler had been tanning himself on a sun-lounger in the garden.

"And didn't he see you?" Ralph asked.

"No, because I was hiding in the bushes by the fence between our two gardens," Thomas replied. "He couldn't see me."

"One of my father's cousins saw a lady friend of Hitler's completely naked," I said. "The cousin lives opposite her, and she's always at her window tanning herself, with her little dog by her side. Her name's Eva Braun."

The bell rang and we went back to class.

Fräulein Weikl talked to us about Hitler again. She told us he wants Germany to leave the League of Nations, the peaceful organization to which countries all over the world have adhered since the war.

"This League is run by our enemies," explained Fräulein Weikl. "It's sucking the lifeblood out of Germany."

Then she read the text of the referendum that was posted up all over the city:

"Do you, German man, and you, German woman, approve this your national government's policy, and are you willing to recognize it as the expression of your own opinion and your own will, and solemnly to profess it?"

■ ■ ■

Mama and I are walking past our local movie theater and the front of the building is covered with referendum posters: Hitler and Hindenburg posing together like Hollywood stars. It's not a movie that's being shown in the theater, the place has been transformed into a polling station and a crowd has gathered by the entrance. A cluster of photographers rush toward a couple approaching the door. The man has a mustache, he's short and pudgy and has a rolling walk, like a spinning top. Trotting along on his arm is a small, older lady, dressed in black and wearing a hat shaped like a flowerpot. Flashbulbs crackle, and the pair step into the building.

The newspaper is open on the table, and I recognize the picture of the couple we came across outside the movie theater. It was Ernst Röhm and his mother. Röhm is commander of the Nazi soldiers, the SA, who are constantly in the streets these days. Fräulein Weikl told us there are now three million SA.

I read the newspaper headline: Over 90 percent of registered voters voted "yes" in Hitler's referendum. Germany will be leaving the League of Nations.

I pray that Rosie's Jesus will protect our family.

*There came a time when I no longer, as in the first days, wandered blindly through the mighty city; now with open eyes I saw not only the buildings but also the people.*

*Once, as I was strolling through the Inner City, I suddenly encountered an apparition in a black caftan and black hair locks. Is this a Jew? was my first thought...*

*I observed the man furtively and cautiously, but the longer I stared at this foreign face, scrutinizing feature for feature, the more my first question assumed a new form:*
*Is this a German?*

—ADOLF HITLER, *MEIN KAMPF,* ON HIS EARLY YEARS IN VIENNA

Hitler has decreed that Munich will be the Nazi capital. He's decided to organize an annual celebration called the Festival of German Art. Soldiers have been going around telling the caretaker in every building what we have to do. Our own caretaker, Funk, came up and told us. He lives in a dark apartment whose windows look out onto the feet of passersby. You can see women's stockings and high heels. Funk and Rosie are great friends so we often drop in to see him on our way back from school, when there's no one at home yet. We sit in the dining room, he gives me orangeade and I listen to them chat. Funk introduced Rosie to politics. He claims "Rosie" is an assumed name in honor of Rosa Luxemburg. Actually, Rosie really is called Rosie. It just makes a better story!

Funk is very short, scarcely taller than me, and he knows how to make people laugh. He's always in blue overalls and seems to be everywhere at once. When you go in through the front door of the building, he's there. When you get home from school, he's in the lobby, bucket in hand. He mops the floor, waxes the wooden stairs and polishes the copper of the banister rail and every door handle in the building. He puts out the garbage and brings up the mail, he takes in the newspapers and hands them around, calling out the headlines. He's always making jokes and teasing Rosie. He knows so much and explains lots of things to us. There are piles of newspapers everywhere in his apartment. He and Rosie talk about Adolf Hitler a lot. Funk knows everything that's going on in the Führer's apartment across the street. He knows the make of all the cars, the names and ranks of the chauffeurs and guards. He was in the war and knows everything there is to know about soldiers. He tells us about generals, corporals, brigadiers, uniforms and their stripes, sabers and rifles, mortars, planes and frigates. He says the SA are just music hall soldiers with no weapons or training, and that the French army is the most powerful in the world.

On a desk in his study he's set out several armies of lead soldiers. His favorites are the Napoleonic forces. They're the handsomest. I like the Grognards best, Napoleon's Old Guard with their tall black fur hats. They look like circus bears.

When Funk talks about historical battles, alliances, kingdoms, republics, emperors, kings and queens, presidents and ministers, Rosie rolls her eyes. She's bored. He stops what he's saying and gives us hot chocolate and a slice of cake. He tells us the Nazis have ordered every inhabitant in the city to light candles in their windows all week. We start lighting ours the very next day. Our neighbors are all doing it too, and there are flags flying from windows, and standards streaming from balconies. My parents say that all these decorations are in bad taste.

"It's like a huge birthday party for a temperamental little king!" my father cries.

■ ■ ■

I woke with a start last night. I heard something that sounded like a drumroll in the street: the storm reverberated through my body as I lay in bed, rain spattered against the windowpanes. There was another, still louder noise, the roar of engines. People were shouting and slamming car doors. I recognized the sound of motorbikes, *Seitenwagen*, which have a sort of carriage on one side, resting on a third wheel; there are more and more of them in the streets these days. I put my head under my pillow and went back to sleep. It wasn't until this afternoon that I found out what happened in the night. Funk and Rosie talked about it at teatime: Hitler went in person to see Ernst Röhm, the fat man whom I saw going to cast his vote with his mother on his arm. Funk said we really need to be careful now. It's dangerous for everyone, not just the Communists, even for the Nazis!

■ ■ ■

I feel uncomfortable. Something important is going on. The duke and Aunt Bobbie have come down to join us. They're here with Papa and Mama, all looking at each other but not talking. The curtains are drawn. We can't see out and no one can see in. Rosie gives me my soup in the kitchen, the door's ajar and I can see the adults in the drawing room. They're just standing there. Papa smooths his mustache with his fingers, the duke adjusts his monocle and offers Papa a cigarette, opening his little silver and leather case where the cigarettes are lined up side by side, held in place by a lever on a spring. Mama and Aunt Bobbie have sat down. All four of them are talking quietly. I catch only the occasional word: "Hitler," "Jew" and "leave."

It's getting dark. The lights haven't been turned on yet in the apartment, it's gloomy, Rosie tells me to finish my soup. She's added all the things I like: cheese, crispy croutons that are now going soft, even a pinch of sugar to cheer me up. When I go to say goodnight in the drawing room Mama's eyes are red, and Papa doesn't even notice

me when I kiss him. I take myself off to bed and Rosie
sings me a song to send me to sleep.

■ ■ ■

We're in Funk's apartment. He's reading out snatches
from the newspaper: "Ernst Röhm was mounting a coup
against Hitler." "He wanted to hand power to the SA,
who would have plundered Germany." "It would have
been chaos." "Revolution." "A bloodbath."

Funk knows everything that's happened. He paces up
and down the room, almost jumping. He's very worked
up, gabbling to Rosie.

"Apparently Hitler caught Ernst Röhm in bed with
another man in a lakeside hotel. It must have been a setup."

"I thought he was a Nazi and very close to Hitler,"
Rosie says. "I don't understand anything anymore."

"Röhm wanted to take things much further than Hitler. He was brutal. The way the Nazis killed him was no
less savage. They're killing each other for power. Ernst
Röhm was shot dead, along with all his companions. He
was given the choice between suicide and execution. He
didn't have the courage to commit suicide."

I don't know what I'd choose if I were asked. We pass
Röhm's house on our way to the park every day. It looks
dead; the garden's strewn with branches and leaves that
fell in the storm. It's like a ghost house. Through the windows you can make out large rooms that look a little
emptier with each passing day. The life has drained out
of the place.

1934

■ ■ ■

I'm now allowed to stay in the drawing room with my parents after dinner in the evening. They talk about their day, open mail, discuss the family. I tell them about school and show them my exercise books. They sign my marvelous drawing, a large swastika, beautifully colored in. I tell them that Ralph's stopped talking to me. I was lonely at first. But I have a new friend now. His uncle is a conductor at the opera house. That's what I'd like to be when I grow up.

In the mornings Rosie and I sometimes walk to Papa's office with him because it's on the way to school. We walk past Hitler's house, along the façade of the opera house, and say goodbye to Papa on the steps to his office building. The people who work there greet him with a "Good morning, sir." He shakes them all by the hand and raises his hat. He makes me laugh: he reminds me of a clockwork toy, always repeating the same gesture. Next Rosie and I walk past a building site just opposite where my dentist is. It's Hitler's project, a big museum devoted to German art. We saw a photo of him in the papers, posing with the architect beside the first stones of the future building.

Papa's at home more and more frequently when I arrive back from school. His writer friends come to see him, and I show them in. I've been doing this since I was very little; Papa taught me how to greet them like a real English gentleman. I open the door and offer to take their hats and umbrellas. Rosie takes care of their coats. Then they sit on the sofa with Papa, and the guests smoke cigarettes. Werner Sombart has a beard exactly like Lenin's, whose picture I've seen in Funk's apartment; Martin Buber looks like a prophet; and Robert Michels wears a black glove on one hand. Papa ensures these guests don't meet each other because they have differing views. Werner Sombart says the Nazis will boost Germany's economy while Martin Buber is no longer allowed to work and is thinking of moving to Palestine. In the meantime he has started writing a new version of the Bible, a superhuman undertaking, according to Mama. Perhaps with his big white beard he actually looks like God. But Carl Schmitt, one of Papa's favorite authors, hasn't visited for a long time. I used to offer him cookies with his cup of tea, and he liked a dash of milk in it, like the English. Mama asks whether he might be ashamed of his former friend and editor because he's a Jew. Papa doesn't reply.

■ ■ ■

To get to the lakes for our vacation this year, we took the train. Laden with suitcases, we squeezed together on the leather seats in the coach.

We shared our compartment with another family. They were all blond. We were all dark. They didn't speak. And neither did we. They had a boy my age, playing with a bag of marbles in his lap. I couldn't see the marbles, but I heard them clinking together. I took my own bag from my pocket and we started talking at last, comparing our agates and taws. He had some I'd never seen and I had some he didn't know. We swapped them. Then we shared our dessert. I had an apple and he an orange. Our mothers helped us cut them into quarters.

His father sat in silence. Papa asked whether he'd like the newspaper he'd finished reading, and the man offered him a cigarette. My father, who doesn't smoke, declined, and suggested they step outside the compartment together so as not to bother the women and children. The little boy, whose name was Karl, and I decided to spy on them. We hid in the corridor. They were leaning out of the window on their elbows, with the wind flattening their hair back. All of a sudden we passed another train and they leapt aside as it whistled shrilly. Their hair was all awry, Papa had ash on his shoulder. Karl and I looked at each other and burst out laughing.

When we arrived they helped us unload our suitcases. Everyone was jolly but it wasn't the end of the line so we had to be quick, the train was about to leave. The stationmaster blew his whistle, the locomotive replied with its own hooting sound, then drew away, hauling the coaches and with them our friends, who waved from the window.

"You see, my darling, we'll just have to get along," Papa said to Mama.

"But what makes you think they're not Jews?" Mama asked.

"He told me they weren't. He's a member of the Nazi Party. He said Hitler's going to sort this all out: he doesn't actually have anything against the Jews, and now that Röhm's off his hands, he's determined to bring those SA thugs to heel."

My father made inquiries at the station. He came back saying that a farmer would take us to Pöcking in his cart. We climbed into a sort of horse carriage. The farmer, an old man with a face as dark and shiny as tanned leather, cracked his whip, and we soon arrived at the villa my parents had rented.

I love being back by the lakes for the summer. We go swimming every day.

One day we stop at the little grocery store on our walk back to the house. The shop's so dark that it takes a while to see anything. On the counter is a display of cheese, butter, bread, canned foods, sausages and jars full of candy. Two children are choosing treats with their nanny. They pay and then leave. I have one pfennig in my pocket and I ask the lady in black for a combination of different candy. She has a head like a mummy, her face all creased. She has a hoarse, bleating little voice and a regional accent. She must be a hundred years old. Apparently, she once met Ludwig II of Bavaria, the Mad King, and the composer Richard Wagner. She remembers when Napoleon died. She hands me a little bag with an assortment of hard candy, *Lutschers* and *Kölnischen Brustbonbons*, along with some sticks of licorice. When I go back outside I'm blinded by the sun. I spot the other children heading off along the pebbly road. The husband

1934

of the old lady who runs the store is standing by the door, talking to my father.

"Poor little things," he says, "Hitler had their father killed with Röhm. Edgar Julius Jung his name was, he used to come here every summer. His crime was writing the anti-Nazi speech given last month by Franz von Papen, one of Hitler's predecessors as chancellor. He was very nearly executed too..."

"Poor little things," Papa agrees.

Later my mother tells him it's risky talking to strangers like that.

"Oh, come on," he says reassuringly, "you know perfectly well the shopkeeper's on our side. His brother's Oskar Maria Graf, the poet. He joked that his only regret since Hitler came to power was that Oskar's books hadn't been burned, because that must mean he's not a good enough poet! Funny, isn't it, don't you think?"

Mama doesn't reply. She seems to be sulking. Papa puts his arms around her and we return to the villa.

Mama's wary of everyone. She whispers in public places and tells me not to talk in front of strangers. I feel we're being watched when we walk in the street. We discuss other people behind their backs too. No one talks to anyone else, but everyone smiles, and we all know everything about everyone. It's a bit like at school, where there are gangs, with bad boys and kind ones. For example, in the next-door villa there's a Nazi musical conductor. I heard Mama saying he's had giant swastikas put up around his opera house. Then she said she won't be going to the opera anymore. In the mornings I see him in his swimming trunks, walking onto the pontoon at the end of his garden. He slips into the water and swims to the middle of the lake. His head grows so small, almost invisible. Then he comes slowly back. When he reaches the shore he doesn't dry himself off right away. He does gymnastic exercises, then a headstand with his head on the ground and his legs thrust up to the sky. I'd like to be a conductor. And I wish I could swim to the middle of the lake.

1934

Gertrud von Le Fort, who has a large villa on the lakes, invites us for a cup of tea almost every day. I find her intimidating because she dresses like a lady in the Middle Ages, always in velvet, with powdery white makeup all over her face that makes me want to cough when I kiss her. She wears red on her lips and green on her eyelids, and her voice sounds like a creaking door. She always has candy for me, hidden in a silver tureen. Mama says she's eccentric, and Papa says she's one of the cleverest women writers in Germany, and perhaps the most interesting of the Catholics. She can claim the Pope himself as one of her admirers. When I tell Rosie about that, I think she's going to faint.

Gertrud von Le Fort sometimes reads to me. She recites boring poems to me, or relates stories from her childhood. In the old days she and her parents traveled for two whole days to reach the lakes. They left Munich hoisted up onto carriages drawn by two oxen. Other carts followed behind, full of trunks packed with hundreds of gowns. They would stop along the way for a picnic lunch, and then set off again. She often fell asleep on a bed that had been set up for her on top of the trunks, snuggled behind velvet drapes. She's liked wearing velvet ever since. Occasionally I read to her too. I've read whole pages from my favorite book, the one I'm reading at the moment, *Robinson Crusoe*. I tell her my plans to go traveling with Ralph someday, to visit Saudi Arabia on a camel. And maybe to set up a new country, like Robinson Crusoe on his island. But Ralph's no longer my friend. I don't know why. Because I'm a Jew, perhaps, and he's a Protestant. Gertrud von Le Fort isn't Jewish either, but *she* listens to me. She's Catholic, like Rosie. She loves Jesus, who was a Jew, and she doesn't like the Nazis. I could tell from the face she made when there was talk of Adolf Hitler at lunchtime.

"We don't talk politics at mealtimes!" she snapped.

I was miles away when she said that and her sharp voice startled me. She noticed, and winked at me.

1935

*Yet I could no longer very well doubt that the objects of my
study were not Germans of a special religion, but a people
in themselves; for since I had begun to concern myself with
this question and to take cognizance of the Jews, Vienna
appeared to me in a different light than before. Wherever
I went, I began to see Jews, and the more I saw, the more
sharply they became distinguished in my eyes from the rest
of humanity. Particularly the Inner City and the districts
north of the Danube Canal swarmed with a people which
even outwardly had lost all resemblance to Germans.*

—ADOLF HITLER, *MEIN KAMPF*

**D**orle is spending her vacation with us in Munich.
The Christmas holidays are here and it's snowing a
lot outside. Dorle sleeps in my bedroom, on a little sofa
that's adapted as a bed. She keeps herself hidden from me
the whole time. When she gets dressed or changes into
her nightdress and dressing gown, she shuts herself in the
bathroom. She's as tall as Mama and has breasts like a

woman, but she isn't allowed to wear makeup or high heels. She wants to be a dancer and often talks about a film she's seen, *The Holy Mountain\**, in which a woman dances the whole time, beside the sea or at the top of a mountain, on the sand or in a blizzard. She shows me how the woman dances, jumping on the bed and then back to the ground. She wants to be a dancer, and a photographer, a mountaineer and a champion skier, to climb Mont Blanc and swim across lakes like Leni Riefenstahl, the actress in the film. Dorle says she's the most beautiful actress in the world, and she may be Hitler's girlfriend.

Over the holidays we stay at home until late into the morning, then go out for a walk. We went skating today. Every winter an open-air ice rink is set up not far from home, between our neighbor's house and Papa's office. A few days before Dorle arrived, Aunt Bobbie took me there to watch a skating performance by the champion Sonja Henie. She's so talented that she took part in the 1924 Olympic Games when she was just twelve years old. She came in last that time but since then she's won everything. Her nickname is "the Queen of the Ice" or "the Pavlova of the Ice." I'm sad that she's Norwegian rather than German.

We've been to the movies several times this week. We saw *Curly Top* with Shirley Temple. She's seven years old and it's her twenty-ninth film. In this one the kids wear dungarees and their hair's all mussed up. They walk around with their hands in their pockets, swinging their shoulders. I copied them as we came out of the cinema.

------

*Der heilige Berg.*

Rosie reprimanded me and Dorle laughed at me. We also went to see a film with Dorle's idol, Leni Riefenstahl. Dorle admires her because she's beautiful and can do everything.

"She's a modern woman," Dorle says.

We went to see her latest film, *Triumph of the Will.*\* It's set in Germany, it could even be just outside our house. It has endless shots of our neighbor Adolf Hitler and crowds of Nazis. The film opens with a plane flying over the city of Nuremberg, which isn't far from here. They fly over rows of SA as tiny as ants, marching through the streets toward the cathedral. Then Hitler lands and everyone cheers. Children my age give him the salute we have to do each morning at school, reaching their right arm toward him, with the palm down and the fingers held tightly together as if for a dive. Hitler barely lifts his arm in response. Perhaps it gets tired from being raised all day long. The film is a talkie and it includes the tune we sing at school, "Horst-Wessel-Lied," which describes the war we'll fight one day, and the glory of the swastika and the Nazi flag. The composer was a young member of the Nazi Party who was assassinated by the Communists in 1930. When we left the movie theater I felt as strong as a soldier, balling my fists in my pockets and walking with my chest puffed out. I could feel the muscles in my arms and chest. If anyone had dared show a lack of respect for Dorle or Rosie, I'd have leapt to defend their honor. Walking through the streets like that, I dreamed I was destined to be a hero. I ran and

1935

_____
\**Triumph des Willens.*

jumped ahead of my protégées on the way home. Back at the apartment Papa pulled a funny face when we told him which movie we'd seen.

I'm fascinated by the newsreels at the movies. Thanks to them, last summer I watched all the ceremonies Hitler arranged to mark Marshal von Hindenburg's death. There were burning pyres, and men with rifles and helmets, holding torches aloft as they escorted the coffin, the whole scene wreathed in a cloud of dark smoke. Thousands of soldiers gathered in a fortified castle, a military procession brought the coffin into the central courtyard and it suddenly disappeared underground. Just then planes flew over the site in formation. A giant flag emblazoned with the Reichswehr cross hung over one of the fortified walls. Standing alone amid the generals and the women in black clothes and face veils was Hitler in his uniform with its cross-belt. He gave the funeral oration and then shook people's hands in the sunshine. The news bulletin also announced that Hitler was now Führer and chancellor, and no one else would be succeeding the marshal. My father coughed out loud and then whispered something in Mama's ear. I hope no one noticed.

■ ■ ■

The holidays are over and Dorle has returned to Berlin. School starts again tomorrow. Lying in bed, I think back over this wonderful week, the films we've seen, and the American and German children we've watched on-screen. I prefer the Germans, but I wouldn't like to have a dagger, a black shirt, a tie and an insignia, and still less join the *Pimpfe* or the *Deutsches Jungvolk*, in which you can enlist from the age of ten—my age. Ralph has the whole uniform, and after school he and some of the other boys do their exercises. On Saturdays they go hiking in the country, and they're planning to camp out one night. I sometimes wonder whether I could leave my family and stop being a Jew, be just German like the others. I'd like to be free to decide who I am and be friends with Ralph again. Maybe we'll be friends again tomorrow.

The school days are long now. It's still dark when we arrive in the morning.

We step through the gates and into a different world. We wait in the schoolyard till the bell rings, then we line up in rows. It's so cold that we exhale clouds of condensation through our nostrils. We're not allowed to put our hands in our pockets. I have woolen gloves but the tips of my fingers are frozen and my feet are icy. My shoes are wet from the snow. However much Rosie greases them in the evenings, nothing stops the moisture seeping into the leather.

We go into the entrance hall and climb the large stone staircase. Talking is forbidden, the only sounds are stifled laughter and the drum of shoes on the floor. Muddy puddles form on the stairs and I always stroke the rabbit carved into the banister rail. On the second floor we turn left toward the classrooms, mine is the first one along the corridor. My desk is by the window, to the side. Lessons begin promptly. I often feel like sleeping, but that's not allowed: if our teacher catches a boy daydreaming, he hurls a piece of chalk at him from the rostrum. It hit a classmate on the cheek once and he stifled his tears but couldn't stop his lips quivering.

We learn Latin and Greek, and I get the two languages confused. But I like learning and luckily I go over my work with Mama in the evenings. When I grow up I'll speak every language, dead or alive, I'll give conferences and be cheered, and when people ask me how I got there, I'll describe the time I spent in this classroom. I must remember everything.

Today our teacher tells us that Saarland has finally rejoined Germany. This small region was previously part of Germany but has been administered by France since 1918. Over 90 percent of its population wanted to be German again, and their wishes have finally been granted. So France is now a little smaller, and Germany a little bigger. And this means there are almost a million more Germans. I'm proud of my country.

"Our Führer has conquered a country without firing a single shot," our schoolmaster says. Then he tells us we must cheer our leader. We all stand up and cry, "*Heil Hitler!*"

The following week our teacher tells us the Führer has decided Germany should have a substantial army, like the major nations. He's going to reintroduce compulsory military service. Then we'll have six hundred thousand soldiers. I look around at the others: they're all smiling to themselves. As we all cheer Hitler again the bell rings, so we put our books away in silence, push our chairs under the desks, and leave without a sound, as we're supposed to. In the schoolyard everyone whoops for joy, except for me.

Ralph and his new friends ignore me, but they're just a small gang of idiots. Everyone else still plays with me. I know there are other Jewish kids in school, although there's nothing to distinguish them. One of them often walks about with his hands behind his back, looking at the ground, like Napoleon; another always hangs around on the school steps, lost in a book, or sometimes he plays alone with jacks or marbles. Every now and then I think my life is sad. Luckily home is wonderful. I adore my parents and Rosie. And Aunt Bobbie too. And the caretaker Funk also, even though he keeps criticizing Germany. I don't know what my schoolmaster would think of that...Funk spoils me, though, giving me candy, comics, color crayons or elastic bands. He makes paper airplanes for me and makes Rosie laugh. We still visit him when Mama's not home yet.

Mama sometimes asks me about our mysterious teas, but I keep them secret.

1935

No one's talking to me. When I arrived home, Papa was sitting at his desk, reading the papers over and over. He smiled at me when I came in, then went back to his reading. Mama came home and I gathered from their conversation that Papa's worried because Hitler's decided to restore compulsory military service. He read an article about this out loud, Mama looked at me, and I thought she was going to cry. Papa reassured her, saying I'm far too young to be enlisted, and that France is bound to stop Hitler equipping himself with his own army.

"No one wants another world war," Papa said.

Now it's nighttime. I've had my bath and my dinner. I'm in the drawing room with my parents, sitting in complete silence. There isn't a sound. I feel lonely. Rosie comes to fetch me to put me to bed, and Mama promises to come kiss me goodnight.

Lying in bed, I'm coming to the end of a book of short stories by Gottfried Keller, *The People of Seldwyla.\** I've got to "The Habit Makes the Monk." In this story, a tailor goes to deliver a suit to an aristocrat in a faraway village. On his journey, the humble tradesman is taken for a nobleman. Instead of admitting his true standing, he puts on his customer's suit and, through a series of adventures, ends up becoming his own prestigious customer, the man he was meant to serve. Would it be possible for me to stop being a Jew?

Mama hasn't come to see me yet, and the sheets are still cold. As I fall asleep, I feel her hand on my cheek. She tucks me in and kisses me. Now I'm dreaming, I think. I dream I can fly through the sky and I'm invincible.

When I get home from school the next day everyone's there, sitting in the drawing room. Papa, Mama, Aunt Bobbie, the duke and Funk. I walk into the room and

---

*Die Leute von Seldwyla*

sidle in among them. An engineer is crouching on the floor, adjusting a large mahogany device with the word "*Blaupunkt*" written on it in gold letters.

"It's a radio," Papa says.

He smiles at me and I can tell he wants me to smile too. He's proud. The engineer lifts the radio's lid. There are lots of wires and two large bulbs. He closes it again and puts the plug into a socket. And all of a sudden there's a crackling sound, then a voice. Adolf Hitler's voice.

"Could you try a different station please?" Papa asks immediately.

The man turns around slowly, peers into my father's eyes for a long time and then looks him up and down through narrowed eyes. He swivels back toward the machine and turns one of the Bakelite dials. A fine line moves across the screen and there are strange sounds. The man turns another pearly dial. The crackling stops and I instantly recognize a piece of music: Schubert's *Hungarian Melody*, a piece that Mama plays on the piano.

1935

Since the radio's been in the drawing room everything's different. Mama plays the piano less, Papa listens to the news, tuning to Radio Luxemburg, a foreign station with programs in German that discuss our country. Its reporters say the Nazis have arrested people who oppose their ideas and have banned newspapers that criticize them. The foreign papers that my father read to me at the Café Stefanie when I was little are no longer sold here, so we listen to Radio Luxemburg the whole time now.

I can now follow the achievements of my favorite sportsmen. The Germans are definitely best at everything. Rudolf Caracciola has an Italian name but he's German and he wins every motorcar race with his Mercedes-Benz W25B. He's an incredible man. His right leg is five centimeters shorter than the left since his accident in Monaco, and he walks with a stick. His wife was killed in an avalanche last year. He's returned to racing and, thanks to Mercedes, he's now faster than his Italian rival, Luigi Fagioli. Hitler ordered the new car for him himself. Thank goodness, because in previous years Caracciola had to drive Italian ones that were nothing like as good! I hear on Radio Luxemburg that this week he won the Tripoli Grand Prix in Libya, in the middle of the desert, by the Mallaha salt lake. I so wish I could have been there among the Bedouin to watch! I picture the desert sand on Caracciola's face, his car powering along at top speed, the roar of the engine, the cloud of smoke on the horizon, pennants waving in the crowd. Last year he reached 311.9 kilometers an hour in a specially streamlined model.

The champion came to Munich in person to deliver Hitler's Mercedes-Benz 770, the gorgeous black car I can't take my eyes off in the street outside our house. Our Führer has announced that he will build *Autobahnen* all over Germany, and people will be allowed to drive faster on them than on the Italian *autostrada*. I really hope so!

The Germans are best at everything. Berlin will host the Olympic Games next year, and our sportsmen will easily win the most medals. I'm sure of it.

Edgar, age three, in the Bogenhausen district of Munich.
In the background is the Kirche St. Gabriel.

Edgar's father, Ludwig, in his study.

Lion Feuchtwanger reading in a canvas chair outside his house in Berlin.
(USC Libraries. Lion Feuchtwanger Papers Collection, 1884–1958)

Edgar (right) with his cousin Ingrid Rheinstrom, in Munich in 1928.

Edgar (right) swimming with his half-sister, Dorle, at a park in Munich in 1929.

Edgar (bottom left), in traditional Bavarian lederhosen,
playing with other boys by a lake near Neuschwanstein Castle.

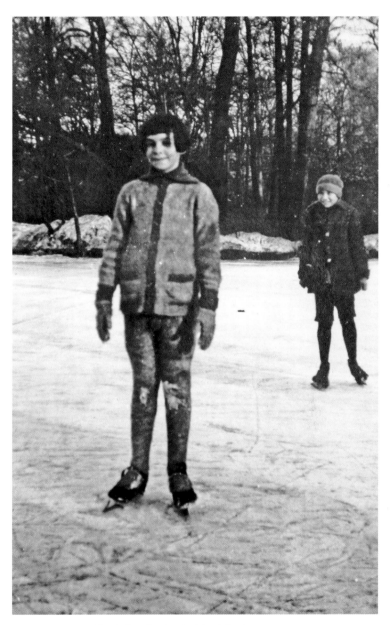

Dorle ice-skating in Munich, circa 1930.

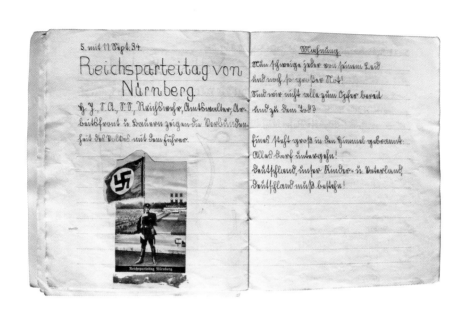

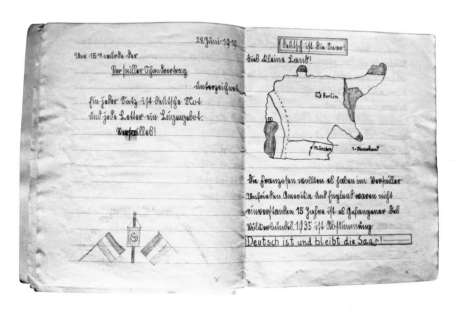

Pages from Edgar's Gebeleschule exercise book, 1934.

Michael Siegel, the father of Edgar's friend Beate, in 1933,
being forced to walk the streets of Munich holding
a placard that reads, "I'm a Jew and I'll never criticize
the police again." (Bundesarchiv)

Hitler on the balcony of his
Prinzregentenplatz 16 apartment, circa 1935.
(Bayerische Staatsbibliothek München/Bildarchiv)

Hitler's Prinzregentenplatz apartment building,
with Nazi banners, circa 1938. (Source unknown)

Edgar in front of Prinzregentenplatz 16, in 2012.

The nasal voice on Radio Luxemburg has announced that France has put up no opposition to Hitler's rearmament. This week the Führer unveiled the prototype of a new warship with a low tonnage, which means it gets around the size limit imposed by the Treaty of Versailles. Even so, it will have far greater firepower than our old ships. The republic's army, the Reichswehr, is to become the Wehrmacht, and Germany will develop its air force, the Luftwaffe, and its navy, the Kriegsmarine. France isn't opposing that either. England has signed a treaty authorizing the development of a German naval force. My father purses his lips, my mother asks him to switch off the radio.

■ ■ ■

1935

We haven't gone for a vacation this summer because my father's traveling to Palestine to visit his sisters. My parents are planning to move there so he's on a reconnaissance trip. I'm getting ready for when we go there: in my room in the evening I study a map of the region, and read descriptions of its cities in the encyclopedia.

During the day Rosie takes me to the public swimming pool. I'm now so good at swimming that I've decided to train for the Olympic Games. I don't know which games, nor for what sport it will be, but I exercise the whole time: I do fifty push-ups in the morning, I run around the outside of the park, and I swim freestyle. I'll be ready soon, people will cheer me on in big stadiums! I'm also doing a lot of reading. I love Adalbert Stifter's stories, romantic fables, like Gottfried Keller's. My favorites are the ones in his collection *Bunte Steine* (Colorful stones), which describe rural life.

I particularly like *Rock Crystal*\*, a story about two children who get lost in the snow on Christmas Eve. The whole village sets out in search of them. They're found just in time, before they die. I enjoy being frightened by it, imagining running away across Germany, alone with only a small dog for company, a few belongings in a bindle, walking through towns and villages, going deep into forests, climbing mountains, building log cabins, making Indian canoes and paddling along rivers all over Europe, traveling upstream to the great capitals: Paris, London...

When Papa comes home from his trip to Palestine, I hardly recognize him he's so tanned. He returns laden with gifts from him and his two sisters, Henny and Medi. He tells us all about it. Henny lives in a large villa in Talpiot, on the outskirts of Jerusalem. She's separated from her husband, Jacob Reich, but they get along so well that they're now inseparable friends. Medi, my father's youngest sister, lives in a little village near Rehovot to the northeast of Tel Aviv. Her husband, Hans Oppenheimer, is a doctor who tends the poor. Papa says they're "gentle idealists" and "Zionist socialists." They have dreams of building the perfect Jewish state there.

"Like Germany for the Germans?" I ask.

---

\* *Bergkristall.*

Mama takes me in her arms but doesn't answer. Then my father uses a map to show us the places he visited: Italy, Rome, Florence, Naples, the crossing to Palestine, arriving by boat in Haifa, then on to Jericho, Jerusalem...He enjoyed his trip and says his sisters are happy there. All the same, he's made up his mind: we won't be going there. Life's too difficult and he's afraid I wouldn't have a good education. And, anyway, he doesn't know what we'd live off. Eventually, Mama's face breaks into a smile, and she runs him a bath. He says there's nothing better than coming home. He turns on the radio and Mama stiffens...

"Not the news, don't worry, darling," Papa whispers.

And we listen to music. An exuberant tune with trumpets.

"But this is jazz!" exclaims Mama, smiling. And Papa kisses her on the lips.

1935

It was the very next day, I think, that we heard the terrible news on the radio. It was in the evening, just before my dinner.

During the big annual Nazi Party rally in Nuremberg—the one filmed by Leni Riefenstahl—Hitler had announced that with immediate effect, Jews would not have the same rights as everyone else.

I wondered whether that would apply to me too.

*Among them there was a great movement, quite extensive in Vienna, which came out sharply in confirmation of the national character of the Jews: this was the Zionist.*

*It looked, to be sure, as though only a part of the Jews approved this viewpoint, while the great majority condemned and inwardly rejected such a formulation. But when examined more closely, this appearance dissolved itself into an unsavory vapor of pretexts advanced for mere reasons of expedience, not to say lies.*

—ADOLF HITLER, *MEIN KAMPF*

R osie's not there when I come out of school today. My mother is instead, standing very upright behind the nannies. She's wearing a fur coat, the one that's so soft I like to bury my face in it and slide my fingers through it. Ralph's chauffeur is waiting by the Rolls-Royce but Ralph doesn't get into the car straightaway, staying to chat with Thomas and Hans. All three of them wear Nazi badges on the lapels of their jackets. They look at me, stare at my mother, and whisper to each other. What are they saying? That she's a Jew? That she looks Jewish? Has a hooked nose? It isn't hooked, she's more beautiful than the other women here, more elegant. And yet I'm embarrassed, I'd rather she weren't here.

Hjalmar Schacht, the minister of economics who was photographed with my parents at the congress in Zurich in 1928, has tried to demonstrate that Jews cannot be completely excluded from the economy. Others have suggested establishing precise categories so that we know once and for all who is a true Aryan—and who isn't. At the moment everything depends on the grandparents' religion. If you have at least three grandparents of Jewish faith, you're fully Jewish. If you have only one or two, you're a "crossbred" Jew or a "half Jew." The Germans have invented a word for this, *Mischling*, which means "of mixed blood."

To find out who you are, you have to find your grandparents' baptism certificates.

Ralph and his gang taunted a friend called Heinrich whose parents had lost their own parents' certificates. They called him a Yid. The next day his parents managed to find the missing documents, and Heinrich coolly ignored Ralph's gang until they came to apologize to him. They've been inseparable ever since and spend the whole of break time comparing their swastika badges.

It's easy in my case. All my grandparents are Jewish—which means my whole family is. That much is clear. Well, not quite. My father's first wife, Dorle's mother, was Catholic. Does that make my sister Jewish like me?

I go to Papa's desk and consult the tables that were published in the newspaper before Christmas. It looks like a family tree and it's very difficult to work your way through all the complicated rules. Only two of Dorle's grandparents are "full" Jews, so she could be seen as a "crossbred" Jew, a *Mischling*. I talk to Papa about it and he says I missed a small asterisk that refers back to the first article in the paragraph: "A person is Jewish if born of an extra-conjugal relationship with a Jew, as defined in article one of paragraph five," in other words "who is descended from at least three grandparents who are racially full Jews," which my father is.

"But she's not from an extra-conjugal relationship!" I protest.

"She is because we're now divorced," my father replies. "I'm no longer married to her mother."

So my sister's a Jew like me.

This time it's my father who's misread. Another condition is tacked on at the end of the article. In order to be Jewish, Dorle would have to have been born after July 1, 1936—so she'd need not to have been born yet, given that it's only January 1936. So Dorle isn't a Jew, then. She's a *Mischling*, a "half Jew." And I'm totally Jewish.

I wish I'd been born in the old days, when my father was young. I'll never be allowed to marry a Catholic, whereas he was free to marry Dorle's mother. If we were caught walking hand in hand we'd be condemned to death for "betraying the race." I remember Arabella and the picnics we used to have together by the lake when we were little. We were just children but I really think I loved her.

1936

I often think of her, her blond hair, her pretty nose and green eyes. I wonder where she is and what she's doing. I'd like to see her again. Her mother comes to the house sometimes, she comes to see Aunt Bobbie. And Dorle? She won't be allowed to love whomever she chooses either. If a non-Jew asked for her hand in marriage—and she accepted—they'd have to get special authorization, and her husband would immediately become a *Mischling* himself, as would any children they had. Who'd want complications like that when for three years now Jews have been denied the right to be doctors, civil servants, news editors, musicians or lawyers? When I go to my dentist, the one I share with Adolf Hitler, the pretty girl with the blond hair and the beauty spot next to her full red lips is no longer there. She was probably Jewish. And what about me? What sort of job will I do and who will I marry?

My mother's waiting for me outside school then. Instead of Rosie. And Ralph and the others are staring at her.

"Why isn't Rosie here, Mama?"

"Come, sweetheart, I'll explain."

"No, Mama, tell me. Why isn't Rosie here? Why didn't Rosie come?"

Mama doesn't answer. She's holding my hand too tightly and frowning.

"Shush!" she scolds. My throat constricts and my eyes sting. The others are watching.

I walk on ahead, on my own. I can hear my mother's footsteps behind me, and the boys sniggering. I start to run, tears trickling down my neck.

I hurry along the familiar route, past the House of German Art, the Nazi Party headquarters, Röhm's villa, Heinrich Hoffmann's, Hitler's apartment, I see our building, climb the stairs as fast as I can, ring the doorbell, Papa lets me in, I bulldoze past him, call Rosie, she's not in the kitchen, or the drawing room, or my bedroom, her room's empty, I scream her name, run back downstairs, ring Funk's doorbell, he opens up.

"Where's Rosie? Where's Rosie?" He takes me in his arms and hugs me. I cry softly.

The Nuremberg laws forbid Jews from employing staff with "German blood" if they are younger than forty-five. Rosie loves me and I love her. Yes, she has German blood—as I did once, before the Nuremberg laws.

I'm a Jew now, just a Jew, nothing but a Jew, nothing else.

All of us are just Jews now, and Rosie's not allowed to live with us anymore.

1936

■ ■ ■

So I'm a Jew then...and the others hate me.

I want to go live in Palestine so that I'm not alone. Papa and Mama talk about it a lot. They gather information, and read specialized books and newspaper articles that Papa obtains from new acquaintances. I listen to their discussions, and look through the books and magazines that they leave open on the desk. I read that this year sixty thousand Jews emigrated from Germany to Palestine, which has one and a half million inhabitants. Many of the new arrivals are from Germany: the German Nazi Party and the Jewish Agency for Palestine have reached an agreement to encourage this migration, which started in the late 1800s. Families from European countries come together and set up colonies on plots of land bought from the surrounding Arab villages. They grow oranges, which are easy to export. These communities are like villages in the South of France, or like the *sovkhozes* in the USSR, where many of these immigrants originated. The young women wear their distinctive low-cut tunics and baggy pants; the men, vests, short pants and peaked caps. Life is overseen by a governing body of seven people, who are elected every year. People work from 5:30 till 11:30 in the morning and 2:00 till 6:30 in the afternoon. No one receives a salary: the colony provides for everyone's needs, not forgetting cigarettes for smokers and instruments for musicians. Every individual has two weeks' paid vacation, and the colony provides them with the money they need for their trip. There's very little organized religion. And each village has a central building where children are raised communally by professional nannies. I wish I were over there and not here.

My father doesn't want to go to Palestine. It's a warring country, he says. Life there is hard. The Arab population is worried by this influx of boatloads of families and thinks these Jews would do better to stay in Europe. Extremists among them ransack shops set up by new immigrants or kill them in the streets, as the Nazis do here. The Jews and the Arabs both have dreams of founding their own country there—and yet Palestine belongs to neither of them, it's still a British protectorate. Many people have visions of creating an independent nation for Jews who can no longer live in Europe, but neighboring countries are against it. If the English ever granted the Jewish nation the right to exist, its neighbors would declare war on it. Jews are known as *Yahud* over there, and they're not allowed into the old city of Jerusalem without risking being stoned. My father thinks the situation will soon be far worse in Palestine than it is in Germany.

"At least we're in Europe," he says. "We can still live among ourselves. We Feuchtwangers are German, whatever they may say, and we have been since 1555!"

My father's told me about our family history: in 1555 my forefathers were driven out of the village of Feuchtwangen, to the north of the Danube, and they moved to Fürth near Nuremberg.

"But we were already here before that!" he adds with still more passion. "We've lived in Germany for more than four hundred years. This madness will blow over like all the others that we Feuchtwangers have survived!"

1936

■ ■ ■

It's already a year since Papa celebrated his fiftieth birthday. I sometimes think about that evening as I fall asleep. All his friends came: the Bernheimers, the Siegels, and every family member who lived in Germany, Aunt Lilly, Berthold, Aunt Bobbie, the duke, and lots of other guests whose names I didn't know. Writers, musicians, people of all ages. The men wore tuxedos, and the women evening gowns. I was dressed like a grown man with a bow tie around my neck. The whole evening reminded me of parties at my cousins the Bernheimers', when my parents used to dance amid confetti, to the sound of a band. On those special nights I would fall asleep in Ingrid's bedroom, lulled by music and laughter. For Papa's birthday, though, I was allowed to stay up till midnight with Beate, who was also there. Her parents looked happy. Her father had only a scar on his cheek as evidence of when he was assaulted in 1933.

Beate and I played at making cocktails for the guests. In the kitchen we poured the dregs from all the glasses into clean glasses, and offered them to the adults, inventing all sorts of fanciful names for these concoctions. I remember one man in particular, he was rather red in the face, unsteady on his feet, and he kept coming back for more.

"Make sure you remember this evening, Edgar," he said, looking me right in the eye.

I thought he was going to cry. My mother appeared and took him off into another room, laughing brightly. Their voices blended with the tune that the band was playing. Before going up to bed, I looked out of the window: the lights were on in Hitler's apartment. He seemed to be alone.

I think I understand what the tipsy man was trying to say. That evening might prove to be the first and last big family party of my life.


My father has stopped going to the office because they've done away with his job. He doesn't go to Café Stefanie either, the place on Kaufingerstrasse where I sometimes went when I was little, and we'd chat with Uncle Berthold, whom I called Bubbi. I remember Bubbi being unconcerned, saying Hitler wouldn't be dangerous. My father no longer goes to Café Heck with its green gardens where Hitler himself once greeted my uncle Lion and Bertolt Brecht. I think back to the days when Rosie and I used to go all the way to Thomas Mann's house to drop off the precious books my father loaned him. It was summertime, I can still picture the dragonflies and butterflies. One time I felt thirsty along the way, and I was allowed to drink straight from the neck of a flask filled with grenadine cordial.

Uncle Lion, Bertolt Brecht, Thomas Mann and so many others have left Germany. Why are we still here?

■ ■ ■

1936

On a sign hanging outside a store I see the words "No dogs or Jews."

■ ■ ■

Papa hardly leaves the house at all anymore. He now works from his desk at home, running a Jewish paper, the *Bayerische Israelitische Gemeindezeitung*. Late into the evening, I hear his big fountain pen scratching across paper, and I can smell his eau de toilette filtering under the doors, all the way to my bedroom. A secretary sometimes comes to note down letters he wants to send. Papa works the whole time, from morning till night, and whether or not anyone's coming to the house, he still dresses as he did when he went out to the office: gray suit and vest, white shirt and a tie. My mother slips silently behind him to bring him a cup of coffee. It reminds me of Rosie, who used to bring him cookies on a silver tray when he was entertaining his writer friends.

Sometimes he travels to different provinces for a few days. He comes back with presents, little porcelain figurines, sliver cups, or glass balls with snowflakes swirling inside them. He gives conferences in surrounding towns and always comes home in a good mood and full of hope for our community.

"No need to set up a nation in Palestine," he says. "Nations and nationalism are a curse, they lead to wars. At the other end of the scale is the human spirit, a spirit of humanity and fraternity, along with culture and knowledge, ideas, thought, music and painting—they know no borders. So the Jews no longer have the right to vote in Germany? Neither do non-Jews because they can vote only for the Nazi Party! At least we Jews can't be their accomplices."

My father opens envelopes with a silver paper knife. He writes letters by hand and sends me out to post them. I run along the street and slip them into the mailbox before the last collection. He gets hold of every edition of the government's newspapers and lets me read them. I'm outraged by the party newspaper, *Völkischer Beobachter*. The worst is *Der Stürmer*, run by Julius Streicher. One headline proclaims in giant letters, THE JEWS

ARE OUR DOWNFALL, and hideous caricatures depict perverse-looking, stooped characters with hooked noses. The Jews are accused of wanting to provoke war in Europe or to steal all the money in the world, particularly in Germany. Four hundred thousand Germans buy this paper every week.

When I look in the mirror I don't see a hooked nose. I don't look like the pictures in the papers. I often think of before, when I was young. I'm twelve now, and I feel so old. Back in the day I was invited to birthday parties. I remember Ralph's party...Does he still like Marcel Proust? Ralph and I wanted to be Spartacists when we were little, we lent each other our favorite books, we wanted to travel the world on camels. No one at school talks to me anymore. The others all discuss the Olympic Games, saying Germany will win everything. On June 19, Max Schmeling beats the invincible Joe Louis at Yankee Stadium in New York and wins back his title as world champion. They say the Aryan conquered the "Negro." They say that the gymnasts Konrad Frey and Alfred Schwarzmann, who fought in the Great War and are now seen as representatives of the superior race, will avenge the German people in the Games.

*1936*

■ ■ ■

I've stopped wanting Ralph to change his mind and be my friend again. It's too late. I'm going to live in my own little world, like my father.

I'm preparing for my bar mitzvah: in the evenings, straight after school, I go to the temple, where Rabbi Glaser teaches religious chants in Hebrew.

Rabbi Leo Baerwald prepares me for the ceremony in Munich's large synagogue. The Nazis have painted swastikas on the pillars that frame the front door. Inside, though, it's a whole different world, calm and peaceful. I like it when children sing with the adults; the younger voices blend with the big booming sound from the grown-ups, it's like angels coming through thunder. They sing in Hebrew and I don't understand a thing, but the music wraps itself around me and transports me. Rabbi Glaser always greets me with a smile, and I join in with the others. I try to decipher the words, pretending to understand them as I sing from memory. I look around, remembering that my father had his bar mitzvah in this same place. He used to put his book and prayer shawl under a bench near the holy ark where the Torah scrolls are kept. I sit on that bench sometimes and think of him. There are fewer than nine thousand Jews in Munich, just 1.2 percent of the population. When the voices grow louder I look down at the floor to hide the tears rolling down my cheeks.


Rabbi Leo Baerwald gives us theology lessons. Today he's asked me to accompany Rabbi Wise, an American, back to his hotel from the synagogue. Rabbi Wise doesn't speak much German and doesn't know the city. We walk in silence. His American suit is more elegant than those worn by passersby and there's nothing to show that he's a rabbi. He's not wearing a *kippah*, just a hat. It's a broad-brimmed hat—a Borsalino, one of my friends told me. I'm happy to be walking along the street with an American. I wish I could go and live there. Apparently there's no school uniform, and children are served milk shakes in drugstores, and people eat pancakes with maple syrup for breakfast, and pupils can take sandwiches to school in little metal boxes. Maybe one day I'll take a boat to New York, where Rabbi Wise lives. He walks quickly, slightly swinging his impressively broad shoulders. I copy him. All of a sudden he stops and shouts something in English. He's pointing at a tram but I don't understand what he's saying. People stop and stare at us; two uniformed soldiers on the opposite sidewalk have slowed down and turned to look at us. Gesticulating to make himself clear, Rabbi Wise asks what's written on the advertising poster on the tram.

1936

It's an ad for the newspaper *Der Stürmer*. THE JEWS ARE OUR DOWNFALL it proclaims, and there's an image of a hideous old man with a hooked nose and clawlike hands. I can't translate it into English. I don't speak his language.

The soldiers cross the street toward us.

"Quick, quick!" I say in English. It's the only word I know. I learned it from the *Mickey Mouse Magazine* that Rabbi Wise brought for the children at the synagogue. Only now does he see the soldiers. We turn around and dive into the crowds. I don't mention the incident when I get back, not to Rabbi Leo, or to my parents. If someone comes to arrest us, I'd rather no one knew it could be my fault.

■ ■ ■

I like learning, and I have good grades. Papa's proud when he signs my school report, which identifies me as an "Israelite." The school stamp is of a large Nazi eagle. The whole city is smothered with swastikas, particularly since the Olympic Games.

The Games took place in Berlin, as planned. France threatened to boycott them, but in the end Léon Blum's government canceled nothing. And yet Blum is a Jew and Hitler had said that German sport was the preserve of Aryans. Opponents of the Nazis wanted to organize their own games in Barcelona, but things have taken a turn for the worse in Spain: with support from Hitler and Mussolini, General Franco now uses cannons to bomb republican towns on a daily basis. So the alternative games were canceled and Spain will soon be yet another Fascist state. Meanwhile, Hitler welcomed athletes from all over the world to the Games in Berlin. They all honored him with a Nazi salute, which is identical to the Olympic salute, with one arm stretched toward the sky. One of the boys at school said it was a sign from God. The Aryan gymnasts Konrad Frey and Alfred Schwarzmann won every event in their discipline. Germany came away with the most medals, eighty-nine as compared to fifty-six for the United States. Leni Riefenstahl is making a film, *Olympia*, to honor our gymnastic heroes who "dominated the world." I've decided not to see it when it comes out.

Standing alone in the schoolyard while everyone else discusses and replays the exploits of our Aryan athletes, I take consolation from the fact that a foreigner, Jesse Owens, won four gold medals right under our neighbor's nose, to his infuriation. The fastest man of all time isn't German. He's American. And he's as black as the black of a Nazi swastika.

1936

*In a short time I was made more thoughtful than ever by my slowly rising insight into the type of activity carried on by the Jews in certain fields.*

*Was there any form of filth or profligacy, particularly in cultural life, without at least one Jew involved in it?*

*If you cut even cautiously into such an abscess, you found, like a maggot in a rotting body, often dazzled by the sudden light—a kike!*

—ADOLF HITLER, *MEIN KAMPF*

D orle has run away. She's disappeared. Aunt Lilly called from Berlin, and for two days now Papa's been calling friends in Lausanne, in Switzerland, where my sister was at boarding school. No one knows where she is. She was meant to go home to her mother for the vacation and instead of catching the night train on Friday evening, she vanished. The telephone rings nonstop. My father's gone silent. He wanted to buy a train ticket to Switzerland but Mama reminded him that without a visa he won't be allowed across the border. He crumpled up a piece of paper in his fist and flung it in the trash.

My father eats his breakfast in silence. His slicked-back hair has gone gray. He still wears a three-piece suit, a matching tie and pocket square and perfectly polished shoes. He purses his lips when he notices something missing from the table. He sets the table more and more frequently to help Mama. A Jewish au pair has replaced Rosie. She's almost the same age as Dorle. Just a little older: twenty-one. Since my father stopped working we have less money, so we give her accommodation and some pocket money in exchange for help around the house. Luckily, I don't need babysitting anymore. Unless I need watching in case I run off like Dorle!

We've had news of the runaway. She left with a boy, a French-Swiss boy called Duvoisin. We're having break-fast and Papa looks so sad. Slices of brioche toast are neatly lined up in the rack on the white tablecloth; steam coils upward from the spout of the silver coffeepot, which stands beside the little milk jug. The raspberry jelly wobbles slightly in the jam pot. Boiled eggs sit waiting to be broken open. Mama's buttering toast fingers for me. She pours me some apple juice and tells me to break into my egg before the yolk hardens. And Papa keeps saying that what matters is Dorle's happiness. He only hopes Monsieur Duvoisin will be kind to her.

■ ■ ■

We're listening to the news. The whole world seems to be becoming Fascist. Anastasio Somoza García is now president of Nicaragua. He's a dictator, like Hitler. Spain's Francoists are still fighting the republicans. Franco's allies the Italians invaded Ethiopia in 1935 and deposed the negus, Haile Selassie. The Italian leader, Il Duce, Benito Mussolini, is to construct a road over a thousand miles long, running along the Mediterranean from Tunisia to Libya. Emperor Hirohito of Japan is forging ahead with his invasion of Manchuria in China. He's appointed a Fascist prime minister, Kōki Hirota, and has recently signed an anti-Comintern pact with Hitler. Meanwhile, in Europe, Britain and France said nothing when in 1936 our troops occupied the Rhineland for the first time since the Great War. The Belgians are worried because this territory is next to their frontier. Germany now has 1,600 aircraft, almost as many as the USSR, which has 2,500, and more than Italy and France. The French president, Léon Blum, has opted to borrow five billion francs to build 1,500 planes before the end of next year. Here in Germany, congressmen in the Reichstag have renewed Adolf Hitler's full power for the next four years. Thank goodness the Americans aren't Fascist yet. President Roosevelt was reelected last year.

"He's not doing anything for us, though," Papa says. "Come, Bürschi, hurry up, you need to get to school."

"But do you think there'll be a war, Papa?"

"Don't you worry. Go on, off you go, my boy."

His hands shake when he pours the coffee. He cut himself shaving this morning. He has more and more little beads of blood on his face, sometimes he misses a few hairs on his cheek. He's been suffering with stomach pains for over a year. He blames the deficiencies in the kosher food his parents used to feed him. I give him a hug and run off down the stairs.

It's cold outside. You can't walk along the sidewalk outside Hitler's house now because there are barriers and, behind them, soldiers standing to attention, watching the Mercedes cars in the street. I recognize the guards because I pass them every day, but they don't notice me, an invisible little Jewish boy. I've been walking past this building all my life, and I watch them closely. I imagine what it must be like being Hitler. I wonder what he eats for breakfast. I see his shadow pass behind a window frame. He hates us. He hates me. Without even knowing I exist.

■ ■ ■

My classmates at school have joined the Hitler Youth. All except me. Well, except us, the Jews. And that's a good thing! Enrollment is compulsory for the others once they turn ten. There was a time when I liked their grand uniforms; now I think they're grotesque. I hear groups of them chattering in the corridors and the schoolyard. All they can talk about is Hitler, and they jeer at the rest of the world, at the French and the English, the Russians and Communists, blacks and Americans. They don't often mention Jews. Perhaps they don't dare when I'm around? After school I can't wait to get home or to my bar mitzvah classes.

■ ■ ■

Last week a friend saw Hitler across the street from the synagogue. He was having lunch at Osteria, his favorite restaurant. He had his back turned but looked around briefly, and my friend recognized his mustache. There were other people at the table, wearing forced smiles. I walked past Osteria yesterday evening, as I left my bar mitzvah class. I'd just been studying the legend of David and Goliath. For a moment I pictured myself going into the restaurant and felling Hitler with a stone hurled at his head from a catapult. I walked on, with my hands in my pockets and my nose buried in the collar of my coat, and went home. I smiled to think he doesn't know who I am. He didn't know that, while he was dining out, a Jewish child was praying he would die—his neighbor who watches him every day and who might well outlive him, the son of a Jew who has no right to work but lives quite happily, the nephew of Lion Feuchtwanger, who continued to defy Nazism from exile in France—the *Republic* of France! I, Edgar, known as Bürschi, son of Ludwig the editor, nephew of Lion the writer, student of Rabbi Siegfried Glaser, I loathed him with all my might without his even realizing it. I scampered home, laughing, whistling and singing. Happy.

Hitler can't do anything about what people think. He can't govern my ideas and see the world going on inside my head. He doesn't know how I feel. We're free in our own homes and in ourselves. At the synagogue we study philosophy; the stories in the Torah are full of twists and contradictory morals. We read them and discuss them, thinking about them in depth in the warm light of our study room. Rabbi Glaser teaches us to think for ourselves but also to embrace everyone else's ideas. The stories are complex and wonderful. I dream I'm David, Moses or Samson. I was born into a cradle drifting on the Nile, my long hair makes me invincible. During these classes, time stands still and I find I'm in Egypt leading a people across seas and deserts, I'm a warrior adored by the masses, striding out under the sun with his hair flowing in the wind. Then I walk home on my usual route, like a legendary soldier protected by invisible armor. The Nazis don't notice me; I watch them openly, no longer afraid of them.

■ ■ ■

Dorle now lives with her Swiss boyfriend in an apartment in Lausanne, and Monsieur Duvoisin has written to my father to ask for his daughter's hand. Papa reads the letter to us solemnly. I think he's going to explode, and he does but not with rage—with joy. Thanks to her marriage, Dorle will have a different nationality and can make a life for herself in Switzerland. Mama thinks she's very young, but Papa doesn't listen to her. In the old days Dorle would have been just the age for a girl to be married and besides, love knows no age boundaries. He adds that we have no choice so we should look on the bright side of things. My father will go to the wedding but my mother's decided to stay here to look after me.

Switzerland wouldn't give us three visas, anyway, for fear we're planning to immigrate there illegally. Papa takes the wedding announcement with him when he goes to ask for a visa from the Swiss consulate. And has no trouble securing one.

It was all over very quickly. My father was back almost before he'd left. It reminded me of when he came back from Palestine. His face was tanned and he brought presents—a Swiss cuckoo clock, Swiss chocolate and Swiss postcards. He described the wedding in great detail and with obvious delight. First came the ceremony at the town hall, then in church. Dorle was dressed all in white. Her husband, a very elegant young man, made the best of impressions on my father. Everyone had dinner in a large restaurant. Papa said that while he was abroad he was struck by how much life here has changed, and he thought perhaps we should all go and live in Switzerland. Five of his eight brothers and sisters have already left: Lion is in France, Henny and Medi in Palestine, and Bella has just moved to Prague in Czechoslovakia, with his brother Martin. Uncle Berthold, "Bubbi," is still here in Munich, as is Fritz. Franziska is in Berlin with her husband, Herr Diamant, and their two children. On my mother's side, Heinrich is in Paris, and we're still sending him parcels of things he left behind. He's effectively moving house by mail! Only her brother Richard is still in Germany, and so is Richard's ex-wife, Lise Bernheimer, and their daughter, Ingrid. Six have gone, four are still

1937

here: more than half of my uncles and aunts have left Germany.

"But Switzerland would never give us three visas in one go," says Mama. "How about Great Britain?"

"We'd have the same problem, and I don't speak a word of English."

"France, then!" Mama exclaims. "We could join Lion."

"But we've already discussed this. With Lion and Marta, there are just the two of them. For the last two years they've been living like luxury tourists in hotels or villas on the Côte d'Azur. They don't have work visas either. They have the same status as every other immigrant with no papers. They're just lucky to have money and a lot of friends. Lion's books have never enjoyed such good sales abroad. Whereas we would have no income."

"It's difficult here too!" Mama retorts.

"But we have a roof over our heads, furniture, books, friends. I'm part of a community here, I give conferences, I run a newspaper. We'd have absolutely nothing there, and we'd be nobodies."

My father grimaces and clutches at his stomach.

"Have you made an appointment with the doctor, my darling?" Mama asks. "It seems to be getting worse."

"Yes, I'm going next week."

■ ■ ■

It's snowed a lot this year, but the winter is over and the weather's getting warmer and sunnier. The tennis courts at the back of our house are open. We can hear balls bouncing, the catgut twang of rackets, the muffled thud of felt on beaten earth. There are no leaves on the trees, just buds, and I watch matches through them. The players, dressed in white, keep score in English. Before, I used to play tennis with my mother. She taught me to serve and come up to the net to volley. We played matches and she kept the score. She'd make me run all over the court, hitting a ball to the right, then one to the left, a long one, then a short one. My shots sailed high in the sky. Hers followed a sort of invisible straight line and I had to run to return them. When was that? During vacations maybe? Or in the afternoons? Rosie used to bring us freshly made lemonade in a wicker-clad thermos...

We're not allowed to play on the public courts anymore.

My father is to have an operation to remove a stomach ulcer. Not very serious, the doctor said, a minor operation. Even so, my parents have decided to send me to Berlin while he convalesces, so that he can really rest. Or for some other reason. I don't know. Aunt Bella's going to take me to Berlin by train, and we'll stay with Aunt Franziska. Aunt Bella lives in Prague. She entered into a "marriage of convenience" to get papers. Her husband—well, her sham husband—is a friend who was happy to help her out. His name's Traubkatz.

*1937*

■ ■ ■

Bella and I are on the Berlin train, sitting facing each other by the window. There are eight passengers in our compartment, four on each seat. I'm the only child because it's not school vacation so children are all in school. My doctor gave me a fake sick note and my parents wrote to my school. They said I have glandular fever, which is a disorder of the blood, and that I need to rest at home. If there's any problem, we'll say I've gone to Berlin for tests. My aunt keeps my papers safe in her handbag, along with the invitation to stay with Franziska. Bella herself doesn't need papers to travel: she has her Czech passport with the name Bella Traubkatz.

This is my first trip to Berlin. At last I'm going to see the German capital. Through the window I watch electric wires rising and falling like waves, from one pylon to the next. Aunt Bella has opened the window slightly because there's a farm laborer in our compartment with hens in a wicker cage. He and his hens smell terrible. The other passengers, all businessmen in suits, are reading the paper in silence. It's funny, they're all holding the same paper, opened wide, sitting with their right leg crossed over the left knee, in identical formation. It's as if there's just one man and his image is reflected in mirrors. I smile to myself as I drift off to sleep.

Aunt Franziska is waiting for us at the station. We follow her through the crowd to a taxi stand where we take a cab to her house. I've never seen so many people in a train station or in the street, or so many cars, shops, bicycles, motorbikes, coaches, trams, buses, young women, children, street peddlers, newspaper salesmen, shops, posters, neon lights, bars, restaurants, banks, cafés, terrace seating, rattan chairs or taverns. There's more of everything.

It's from here in Berlin that Hitler is threatening the world. And yet the capital feels less Nazi-influenced than our little city of Munich. The sidewalks aren't stiff with SS officers or children in uniform. I don't see any caricatures of Jews on the sides of buses, or racist posters.

Aunt Franziska's apartment is similar to ours. It's huge and warm, full of books and adorned with paintings. I'm staying in the younger child's room, Bella in the elder's. It's the first time I've slept alone far from my parents. Before going to bed this evening, Aunt Bella told me about her life in Prague. She said she's free, as she used to be in Germany, free to live the life she chooses, and she feels sure that someday we'll all meet up in Prague or somewhere else. We can live together, happy and carefree, her brothers and sister and their friends, including my parents and me. She sat on the edge of my bed and talked to me in the dark. I could hear the smile in her voice, and her eyes were bound to be shining as she described her happy childhood in Munich and her memories of school, she even mentioned the names of friends she played with when she was my age. She described the people in Prague, where Jews are seen as ordinary citizens. With her passport she can travel all over the world. She was very persuasive: we must get visas, and then passports for another country, any country, and we must go, leave Germany as soon as possible, before it's too late. I lay there for a long time listening to her singsong voice as she described the world she lives in, the shops where she buys her clothes, the restaurants she goes to, and others she'll visit in the future, in Paris, London and New York.

I pictured the life she'll lead, and I imagined her getting married in a long white dress. I felt her hand on my cheek and her lips on my forehead in the warm darkness.

Aunt Franziska is caring and attentive. When we arrived yesterday, the dinner table was already set. She served us cold meat and sauerkraut. Then when she showed me my bedroom, the bedsheets had been turned back specially for me, my clothes put away in the dresser, my toilet case waiting on the shelf above the basin in the bathroom, my toothbrush out ready.

Breakfast this morning is served in the living room. I arrive wearing the bathrobe provided for me, it was waiting for me, folded on my bedroom chair. The three of us—Bella, Franziska and I—have breakfast together. I haven't seen Franziska's husband, he came home late last night and has already left for work this morning. Although he's a Jew, he's allowed to continue his business deals in Berlin.

I'm happy to be here. There are sounds of car horns from the street and the trundle of buses and trams. I can't wait to go out. Someone rings at the door and I immediately recognize a voice: it's Aunt Lilly, my father's first wife, Dorle's mother. I run out into the hall and hug her.

"You just wait, my little Edgar, my Bürschi. The two of us are going to have such fun without your parents and without Dorle now she's married. Did you know she's having a baby? No? Well, it will be born in six months. And here am I all alone, or almost. There is Lewandoski. Well, I'll explain. In fact, he has a candy factory—imagine that! And you just so happen to be invited to go visit! Isn't that wonderful? Oh my, how you've grown…"

I hug her close and breathe in her perfume, the Parisian perfume she's always worn; I've known it all my life from when she's held me in her arms like this. She takes my shoulders and stands back to look at me, she ruffles my hair with her hands, then straightens it and hugs me again. She's wearing makeup. With her red lips, blue eyelids and over-powdered face, she reminds me of the paintings I saw at my cousins the Bernheimers', Toulouse-Lautrecs, Manets or Monets, I don't remember now, I get them all muddled up. She looks like those women from the last century whose dresses are full of lace, their hats decorated with real flowers, their lips red and their eyes heavily made up. I notice her breasts barely covered by a silk wrap. Embarrassed, I huddle against her and look away.

■ ■ ■

Berlin is like paradise. I don't feel Jewish here. I've spent the whole week with Aunt Lilly. We visited the factory owned by Herr Lewandoski, her fiancé, and when we arrived he ran down the staircase to the doorman's hut where we were waiting. He kissed Aunt Lilly's rings, making her laugh like a child, then showed us up to his office, which is made entirely of wood. It's modern art, he told us. The bookshelves, cupboards and mirror frames looked as if they'd been sculpted from a single piece of highly polished oak. I thought of the advertising posters for big transatlantic steamers. The room was like a large cabin on a ship. Then we had our factory visit, and everywhere we went men in blue coveralls greeted Herr Lewandoski. We reached the machine room dominated by great steel vats filled with a bubbling concoction that would produce candy. Sugar is transported to the vats in huge paper sacks and these sacks are emptied into metal chutes. The sugar spills into the vats, and mechanical arms combine it with water while the temperature rises. Then it undergoes a complicated journey through tubes, along conveyor belts and over steel slats positioned by operators—in white coveralls this time—who monitor needles turning on dials. At the end of this journey a long black, white, blue or red paste emerges. Other machines cut it up and women package the candy in pretty paper wrappers decorated with the factory's logo. When I came away my pockets were bulging with candy. Aunt Lilly walked like a queen and the workers looked away out of respect.

In the course of a week we've explored the whole city on foot, by tram or by taxi: the Brandenburg Gate, the avenues, the museums. We visited Frederick the Great's Palace in Potsdam. I had a Viennese hot chocolate in a café where a band was playing: jazz, Aunt Lilly told me. We watched an American film, a musical. Then Aunt Lilly and Aunt Franziska took Bella and me to the station, the vacation was over. That was when I remembered Papa was ill and we had to go back to Munich, where school would be waiting for me. My old life would start again, opposite Hitler's house.

■ ■ ■

The apartment is dark. My mother's playing piano and the door to my parents' bedroom is ajar. My father's in bed asleep, his hair awry. He looks like an old man. He hasn't got up for a week. I bring him his supper on a tray and sit beside him, but he doesn't talk. A smell of medicine hangs over the whole house. It's gray outside and raining. The tune my mother's playing is ominous, gloomy. I can hear the floorboards creak and the wind outside. I don't like going to school anymore, but it's worse at home. I'm bored, my parents are sad, I don't have any friends, or brothers and sisters, I'm alone. The au pair's hardly ever here. In the early days she talked to me and told me her secrets. She wanted to meet a young man, get married, have children, she dreamed of meeting a Catholic, or maybe a Protestant, so her children wouldn't be Jewish, like her—"But Protestants are the worst anti-Semites," she confided another time. She now has a fiancé and doesn't tell me anything. All I know is he's Jewish.

1937

Their children's lives will be as miserable as mine.

I hope my father isn't going to die.

■ ■ ■

Papa's condition has improved. He's himself again. He works as much as he did when he was running a building full of offices, bellowing all day long, dictating letters to a woman who comes more and more frequently, and sending me out to the letter box. He gets angry, issues orders, makes telephone calls. I picture our neighbor busying himself too in his office on the other side of the street. I wonder which of the two gets the most done. Of course Hitler's running a whole country, he changes laws, initiates new directives, barks on the radio, pretends to consult Il Duce in Italy, coaxes the French prime minister, Pierre Laval, stands up to Joseph Stalin, instigates huge building projects, has freeways built so he can travel faster from his apartment to his Eagle's Nest in the Alps, rearms the nation, gathers huge crowds, appeals to old ladies and young girls, and never stops coming and going in the street outside our house. But my father has a new idea every second too. He scrawls them on blocks of paper, corresponds with writers, broaches new subjects for his newspaper, writes letters of complaint, calls lawyers and intellectuals who are acquaintances of his, some still working, others retired, gulping down a bowl of soup brought to him on a tray, a pencil behind his ear, the telephone receiver wedged between his shoulder and his neck. He's toiling against Adolf Hitler, "while there's still time." The people he writes to are in Palestine, London, Paris, New York, Lausanne, Rome and Berlin. He starts going out into the city again, meets his contacts in parks. What if it were possible? What if the Führer could be brought down? When I wake in the mornings he's already up. He barely looks at me over his glasses, kisses me absentmindedly, then dives back into his international newspapers. He comments on the news to my mother and tells her how he plans to influence events. Then he writes to everyone he knows, from the now Nazi and all-powerful Carl Schmitt, who was an author of his and so loved it when I served him tea, down to his own brothers, the eldest of whom, Lion, has actually recently met Joseph Stalin for a proposed book.

"I read his interview with Stalin in the paper, and I know exactly how he'll write his book!" he roars at Mama. "But he's wrong. Stalin's no Father of the People— oh, the naivete!"

When my father leaves the house with his hurried purposeful step, wearing a suit exactly like those our neighbor wears—when Hitler's not dressed up as a general, that is—I imagine them fighting it out hand to hand, and wonder which of the two would prevail.

■ ■ ■

It's my bar mitzvah today. I'm standing alone at the bimah. There are benches to the left of the door with men sitting on them, my father in the front row. On the right are the women, including my mother. The synagogue is full but I don't recognize the faces. I intone the sacred texts taught by Glaser, with my father watching me. He's promised me that from this day on I'll be a man.

1937

*I didn't know what to be more amazed at: the agility of their tongues or their virtuosity at lying.*

*Gradually I began to hate them.*

—ADOLF HITLER, *MEIN KAMPF*

We've stopped celebrating Christmas. My parents used to want me to believe in Santa Claus, like other children; Rosie would be busy for a whole week, cutting up paper decorations and felt in every color. She and Mama hung holly on the door and ribbons at the windows. It all seems so long ago! On my way home from school recently I've seen people hurrying through the cold, eager to get home to their family gatherings. Through those candlelit windows I spied trees hung with garlands and baubles.

The lights are all on across the street too. Who's he with? Maybe he's alone, because he has no family. Or with the housekeeper, Frau Winter, whose name appears next to the doorbell instead of his. His SS guards are doing their usual rounds. I recognize every one of them. The full moon picks out their black uniforms, the gleaming leather of their visors and boots, the glossy paintwork of their cars. They melt into the darkness with its smattering of stars. Shadows hover behind the curtains on the second floor, in his home, in that fateful apartment where, in 1931, his niece Angela Raubal shot herself through the heart with a revolver. There used to be all sorts of rumors about the Führer's love affairs, and foreign journalists chronicled his life in papers that were by then banned in Germany. I still remember my parents talking about it in the evenings when they thought I was asleep. I think this niece, who was nicknamed "Geli," was his girlfriend. She was his half sister's daughter, and he hasn't lived with another woman since. They say the girl's room has been left just as it was the day she died. They also say she didn't call him "*Mein Führer*" because that wasn't yet his title. What did she call him? "*Mein Onkel*" perhaps, "Uncle Adolf" or maybe "Alf," a diminutive of "Adolf"... I don't know. People say he loved a girl called Jenny, the sister of one of his drivers, then Erna, a friend's sister. He allegedly courted Henny, the daughter of his photographer Heinrich Hoffmann, whose house I know; then Richard Wagner's daughter-in-law, Winifred. He may have contemplated a relationship with the Englishwoman Unity Freeman-Mitford. But in the end all these women married other men.

When I was little my cousins told me they'd seen one of his women friends naked at the window of his apartment. She was his photographer's assistant, still the same photographer, Heinrich Hoffmann, who displays images of the Führer in his shop window. Then there was Dorle's idol, Leni Riefenstahl, who tired of him—or perhaps he was the one who left her, when he realized one of her grandmothers had Jewish blood. Despite his successes with women, he still lives alone. And yet, every Wednesday, a bevy of twenty girls comes to have lunch with him. They're sometimes seen arriving in traditional costume. Rumor has it that the girls sit at one table and he at another, eating his potatoes and vegetables alone. At concerts a spare seat is always left next to him. Hitler claims he has only one partner: Germany.

He must be alone this evening, then. His window glows at the end of the street. Does he have a Christmas tree? We don't.

All week Mama's been leafing through magazines, looking at advertisements that rave about the delights of palaces on the Italian Riviera, in San Remo or Campione, or on Lake Lugano. One has its own casino where you can play roulette, baccarat or thirty and forty. In the ballroom they put on operas, plays, reviews, symphonies, ballets, attractions and receptions. It has an eighteen-hole golf course. The advertisement says it is "Unique in Europe for the sheer quality of its club, restaurant and entertainment." My mother lingers greedily over a photo of a young woman trying out an "inimitable" lipstick. I myself would love to have a mechanical pencil or a fountain pen where you can see the ink level and with a little reserve tank, or a "Kodatoy" for projecting real movies at home. If my parents had driving licenses we could buy a car, a racing car! On a salt lake in an American desert, a British driver called

Sir Malcolm Campbell is hoping to break the 300 miles-per-hour barrier at the wheel of a car named *Blue Bird*. It will have a Rolls-Royce engine and could reach speeds of 350 miles per hour. I'd so love to see that machine!

It's Christmas tomorrow but I may not have any presents. Dorle's had her baby now and won't be with us this year. Our au pair has gone to have dinner with her fiancé's parents. The three of us are here alone. We eat in silence, the only sounds the clink of cutlery on our plates and noises reaching us from outside. Mama has forbidden listening to the radio during meals and Papa doesn't want us to talk politics. Which means no one says anything. I'd like to go to bed. Since my bar mitzvah I feel there's no sense in celebrating Christmas: it's not a religious festival, nor a traditional one because we Jews are no longer seen as part of the German nation. What's the point in pretending?

December 25 was just an ordinary day, with no presents. Our days are dreary and insipid. Any pleasure in life has evaporated. No one talks to anyone else in the building now. I've stopped going for tea with Funk, and he's stopped coming up to our apartment. Aunt Bobbie hasn't been to see us for a long time. There are rumors circulating, they reach us like the icy January wind that sneaks under the window.

In Dachau camp, men are penned together by category. The Communists on one side, Catholics on the other, homosexuals in one bunkhouse, Gypsies and Romanies in another. Jews who complain are arrested. Some people say they're killed, others that they're not treated as badly as all that. Whom to believe?

"And anyway," I overhear an old lady telling her friend in the street, "Hitler's been in prison himself! And he didn't come off all that badly: he said it was better than university and he wrote *Mein Kampf*. So then? Why make such a fuss about everything?"

■ ■ ■

My parents argue and keep changing their minds. One day one of them says we should leave and it doesn't matter where we go, then the very next day they agree there's nowhere we'd be any happier than here. One hundred and twenty thousand Jews, that's one in five, have already left Germany. My mother wants to go to France or England.

"A Jew can rise up to be prime minister there," she says. "And twenty-five thousand of us have already settled there."

"My darling," my father replies flatly, "most of them  left without visas, terrified they'd be interned, Lion wrote and told me about it. And you must never idealize anything, you know that. Don't forget that modern anti-Semitism was born in those countries: in France it was an unstable character called Joseph Arthur de Gobineau, then in England it was another madman, Houston Stewart Chamberlain. He's the one who came up with the theory of the Aryan race. Adolf Hitler took his inspiration from him, conveniently forgetting that—according to his beloved Chamberlain—the Germans weren't actually part of it."

My father would rather immigrate to the United States.

"Fifteen thousand of our people have just emigrated there," he adds to bolster his argument. "It now has more Jews than any other country in the world: four and a half million. They say one in every four New Yorkers is Jewish."

My father doesn't know how to get visas for us. As he does every evening, he goes back through the list of countries where we could live.

"In Poland, where there are three million Jews, that's ten percent of the population, they're bullied the whole time. There are only two hundred thousand in Austria but it's much worse there. In Russia there are as many as two million seven hundred thousand and they're being massacred—and it's a Communist country. In Spain there are four thousand, but there's a civil war going on."

My parents agree that the worst place would be Palestine. They read all sorts of publications that print our people's statistics: there are 15,800,000 Jews in the world; 38.6 percent work in commerce, 36.4 percent in industry, 6.3 percent exercise a profession, 4 percent work in agriculture, 2 percent in domestic service, and 12.7 percent live off private incomes, are pensioners or in care.

"How on earth can you trust figures like that!" my father cries.

And nothing happens. I go to school and come home. Our neighbor keeps up his peregrinations: at home one day, in Berlin the next, then in his chalet in the Alps, the Eagle's Nest. We hear him shrieking on the radio every evening. I sometimes come across him in the morning. As our world gradually shrinks, his expands. And I keep escaping inside my own head, reading, dreaming, traveling in my thoughts.

■ ■ ■

The House of German Art, opposite the office of the dentist we share with Hitler, was completed last year, while I was in Berlin. Since then it has exhibited paintings by artists accused of perverting the noble German spirit with their "degenerate art." My mother has been to see them, knowing she'll never see such a concentration of paintings again. She described the line of people waiting that stretched the full length of the colossal building, and she told me about works by Dadaists, cubists, expressionists, fauvists, impressionists, surrealists and futurists, original works by artists I'd so often heard my parents discussing, Marc Chagall, Max Ernst, Paul Klee and Pablo Picasso.

That same week our city celebrated the annual Spring Festival. Vintage floats moved in a procession through the streets, and girls in vestal virgins' tunics scattered flower petals on the wind. Mama and I watched them go by, leaning on the windowsill, half hidden behind the awnings we put up every year for the Festival of German Art. Young men dressed as Roman citizens, wearing Spartan-style sandals, walked soundlessly in the gentle warmth of early summer. A pastel blue sky tended toward light pink. In my

1938

mind this memory has become confused with my mother's descriptions of the paintings she saw. On the other side of the street, at the balcony of the building opposite, where the outstretched arms of those moving past converged, I saw our neighbor's silhouette.

Although he's Austrian by birth, Adolf Hitler is running Germany. He grew up in the country and then studied fine art in Vienna, a place I've never visited. He wanted to be a painter, like the duke whose paintings adorned every wall of Aunt Bobbie's apartment. I remember the duke allowing me to add to one of them with a paintbrush loaded with paint. He encouraged me to dip it into the color of my choice and put a smudge onto the impressionist work he was painting. Like the duke, and like all "degenerate" artists, Hitler enjoyed painting landscapes. He made artist friends in Vienna, some of them of Jewish faith. It was still in Vienna, after his mother died—he had already lost his father—that he experienced his first failures: he was poor and his work had little success. My father ascribes the reason for his violence to these humiliations. That would make Vienna the true cradle of Nazism. And the pro-Hitler crowds there are even more fanatical than here. For several days now, everyone's been talking about Austria: my classmates, radio presenters, the newspapers that salesmen sell with loud cries in the street, my parents at home and passengers on the tram...world leaders are talking about it too.

When I arrived home today, my father was chatting with a stranger in his study. They turned around when I opened the door.

"My son," Papa said, without introducing the other man. He was a very tall man and struck me as particularly elegant. His long slender hands rested on his long, crossed legs.

"Hitler wants Austria and Germany to be reunited," my father continued with their conversation, "as they used to be. He wants to annex Austria. He managed to do it with the Rhineland, and plenty of Austrians have converted to his megalomaniac opinions and share the fantasy. Mussolini used to oppose the idea—but no longer does. In fact, he seems to adhere a little more to our chancellor's vision with each passing day: in Italy Jews no longer have the same rights as other citizens, just as they don't here. France, Great Britain and the United States are officially against this annexing. But they did nothing when the Führer seized the Rhineland. Why would they react this time?"

I slipped away to lie on my bed and read. When I heard the door click shut a little later, I knew my father's workday was over. And went back to my reading.

1938

■ ■ ■

In the night I'm woken by a rumbling sound again.

I once read that during an earthquake buildings sway, chandeliers swing and sometimes fall, windows break and shatter on the sidewalk. When the earth shakes like that, houses crumble, disintegrate and collapse, and so do larger buildings, and churches. On the night of June 30, 1934, when the SS deposed the SA and Adolf Hitler had Ernst Röhm arrested in his bed, the windowpanes in my bedroom shook, and I remember seeing raindrops accelerating down the glass. I got up to watch the soldiers busying in the street below, preparing cars. The roar of engines woke the neighborhood and people clustered at windows. On the other side of the street, the Führer's apartment was lit up like a searchlight through the mist. I didn't see him come out of his building or slip in beside the driver of his sedan and give the order to leave. The posse set off toward the lakes making a noise like thunder.

This morning the windows are shaking to a metallic rumbling intercut with snapped orders, tired hoarse voices, the thunderous thrum of cars and the sputter of motorbikes. It's like the night of June 30, 1934; the lights in the building opposite come on, and, hidden behind the curtains, silhouettes in other houses watch the corner of the street. On the left-hand side at the end, by Prinzregentenplatz, there's a rotunda-shaped building, and behind the balustrade on the corner of that building, right where his living room is, his study, his bedroom, the lights are on too, as they are in everyone else's house. Soldiers dressed in the characteristic caps and straps of their green uniforms load things into cars. I see my mother and father, now awake, watching furtively through a veil of tulle. All of a sudden, in an unimaginable blast of backfiring, one, then two cars, then the whole detachment sets off and disappears in a cloud of black smoke at the end of the street. The noise is still ringing in my ears. My mother buries her face in the crook of my father's arm. I cling to them both. I feel Papa's fingers in my hair, he strokes the back of my neck and I close my eyes.

■ ■ ■

A few days ago, on Saturday, we invaded Austria. Our troops crossed the Austro-Hungarian border and went all the way to Vienna. The Austrians welcomed them with flowers and Nazi flags. Chancellor Kurt von Schuschnigg offered his resignation to the Austrian president, Wilhelm Miklas, who accepted it. Papa spoke von Schuschnigg's words, imitating him in a mocking, nasal voice:

" 'We surrendered because we refuse, even in this most terrible hour, to shed blood. And so we decided to order our Austrian troops to offer no resistance.' "

Papa tells us that the leader of the Austrian Nazi Party, Arthur Seyss-Inquart, has been appointed chancellor. He gives us a summary of events drawn from what he's read and from reports by his contacts in Austria, Berlin, London and Paris. It's like a film. Standing at the front of the six-wheeled Mercedes-Benz G4 that we saw set off in the drizzle, Hitler reached Brannau, the village where he was born, at 4:00 p.m., drawing into that little border town on the Austrian side of the River Inn, where his father once worked as a customs officer.

"They definitely have a thing about borders in that family!" my father is moved to say.

Hitler continued on his way. At 7:00 p.m. he was in Linz, the place where he went to school from the age of

*1938*

nine to sixteen. That evening he stood on the balcony of the town hall overlooking the central square and was greeted with cheers. The next morning, on Sunday, he stayed in the Linz of his teenage years, visiting his childhood home in Leonding and laying flowers on his parents' grave. On Monday he was back at the front of his car, sitting this time, bolt upright and with his arm raised, traveling through Melk and Sankt-Pölten, where the crowds chanted his name and waved little Nazi flags. He reached the Imperial Residence at 6:00 p.m.

"Never again can anyone divide the German Reich as it is today," he announced from the balcony.

The next day, two hundred and fifty thousand people came to listen to his speech in Heldenplatz. Austria was to become a province of Germany, with the name "Ostmark," and Arthur Seyss-Inquart was appointed as its governor. Earlier in the day, the Führer had visited the grave of Geli, his niece who committed suicide in his apartment. A simple wooden sign on her grave bears the words: "Here lies our beloved Geli in her final sleep. She was our ray of sunshine. Raubal family." During the course of the day Viennese Jews were dragged out in front of their ransacked shops and made to kneel before passersby who shouted, "Death to Jews!"

■ ■ ■

He came straight back to Munich. Barriers had been set up all the way from the train station to the street outside our house for his return. Through the window we saw the procession approach from far in the distance, and eventually stop outside his building. I was amazed to see so few people gathered to watch. It was a far cry from the tides of humanity in Austria that were still appearing on the front pages of all the papers.

■ ■ ■

It's nearly a month now since Austria was annexed. The British prime minister, Neville Chamberlain, said this was not "a moment for hasty decisions or for careless words," adding that "we must consider the new situation quickly, but with cool judgment."

"And he didn't do a thing," Papa says. "No more than the French or the Americans did."

A referendum was held in Austria and Germany. In answer to the question "Do you approve of the reunification of Austria with the German Reich that was decreed on March 13, 1938, and do you vote for our leader Adolf Hitler's party?" 99.08 percent of Germans replied "yes." The Austrians were even more convinced, with 99.75 percent voting "yes."

People are saying that in Austria Jews, Social Democrats, Christian Democrats and Communists are being arrested and sent to camps; others are transported to Germany and imprisoned in Dachau, near Munich. What becomes of them? How long will they be held? How are they treated? Their families have no news. Foreign newspapers report on the annexing of Austria, and major leaders worry about possible plans for other conquests.

And no one ever does anything about us. Yesterday was German Art Day. As they do every year, men and women in costumes from past ages—representing the evolution of the Aryan race—processed through the city's streets. On the same day the Nazis finished demolishing our synagogue.

"It bothered Hitler. Having that building so near the Osteria gave him indigestion, and just turning his back on it while he ate wasn't enough of a remedy," Papa quips.

We go to see the remains. There's nothing left of it. Just a great gap. A space where my childhood memories once were. This place is no longer our country, so why don't we leave? I have no one left to talk to at school. I arrive in the morning and leave in the evening. I study in the classroom, and read by myself in break time. I don't want to be identified, or even seen. I'm invisible. Ralph and the others don't notice me anymore. I'm never called to the front of the class. Soon I'll be transparent, I won't look the other students in the eye, or the teachers. In gym I used to be fastest at climbing a knotted rope. I've deliberately slowed down so I no longer come first. I want to be forgotten, nonexistent, until we leave for real, and go to Chile, Cuba or Argentina, the only countries that accept Jews—on condition we pay for our visas.

A friend of my father's, an Argentine diplomat, says we must leave at any price, he says the Nazis and Fascists will take power in every country on the European continent, and soon Jews will be in danger everywhere. The papers are saying that in England the masses are being seduced by the far right too.

"In that case," my father replies, "could the United States tip the same way?"

And this friend with the foreign accent, who rolls his *R*s like a Bavarian, who has dropped by my father's study this sunny afternoon, replies simply:

"Why not…"

■ ■ ■

Hitler has decided that soon every German will have a car. Every Nazi, to be precise. Party members can already benefit from this plan. You have to be affiliated with the KdF, Kraft durch Freude, which means "strength through joy." This organization is part of the DAF, the Deutsche Arbeitsfront, a state-run body that has replaced the unions disbanded on May 1, 1933 — I remember that day, our teacher made us draw a picture, and I have a feeling Mama's kept it somewhere: it was a swastika in front of a hammer, and it represented Nazism's superiority over Bolshevism. The KdF arranges almost-free vacations for its members, and twenty-five million Germans have already benefited from this. Not a single Jew, of course.  Papa says he'd have to be paid to go spend time in their centers: people are accommodated in big characterless buildings, and they spend their days around undersized swimming pools, roasting in the sun. You even have to join in group gymnastics sessions. The *Wilhelm Gustloff*, a newly completed ship, has been made available to the organization so that every German can go on a cruise once in his or her life. It's a liner more than 208 meters long and 23 meters tall—the size of our apartment building. If it dropped anchor outside our house it would take up the whole street. We could meet Hitler on the bridge, halfway between our apartments.

So the KdF is offering a car to each of its members: a KdF-Wagen. It's rounded like a beetle and looks like an aircraft. It can transport four people at more than one hundred kilometers an hour and will cost less than 1,000 marks—990 exactly. Hitler himself designed it on the tablecloth in a restaurant, the Osteria, I think; and Ferdinand Porsche, a former Mercedes engineer, put it together to match his instructions. Porsche worked in the United States, where he studied production techniques perfected by Henry Ford, a friend of the Führer's. Members of the KdF can already open an account and pay 50 marks into it every week. When the contract comes full term, their vehicle will be delivered. They'll have to add just 50 marks extra for the delivery. By then thousands of kilometers of *Reichsautobahnen* will have been constructed. The car can have a roof with an opening or can be a convertible. Its revolutionary engine is at the rear of the chassis, and the interior has a quasi-aeronautical design inspired by the cockpit of a plane. We have a sales brochure at home that explains it all. It has a picture of Hitler celebrating the delivery of the first model before a crowd of young men in uniform. There are also pictures of large clean factories and a color image of a KdF-Wagen climbing a twisting mountain road. Sadly, we'll never have one, because membership in the KdF is forbidden to Jews. What if we left Germany one day? I'd so love to live somewhere else…

■ ■ ■

"When Chamberlain takes a vacation, he goes to another country. When Hitler goes for a vacation, he takes another country."

My father collects amusing stories about the Führer. He says they come from London—I think he's making them up. Strangely, I feel as if the sadder he is, the funnier he is. The smaller our world becomes, and the more isolated we are, the more laughter there is at home.

■ ■ ■

For some days now there's been talk of invading Czechoslovakia, where Aunt Bella lives. This foreign country that borders Austria—which is now Germany—is home to half a million German-speaking people of German origin, descendants of German workers brought in by Bohemian kings in the last century. They mostly live in the Sudeten and Carpathian Mountain regions. Hitler, who's Austrian by birth, deems them to be entirely German, just like himself, and this view is shared by members of  the Czech Nazi Party. "On the weekend, when Daladier might like a spot of camping, Hitler goes in for a spot of campaigning," my father remarks when he reads in the papers that Hitler's now calling for Czechoslovakia to be annexed in order to "liberate the Germans in the Sudeten Mountains from Czech oppression."

"Look, darling," my father jokes, "our friend Adolf is going to play the same trick as he did with Austria. Konrad

Henlein, the puppet leader of the Patriotic Front of Sudeten Germans…Oh, no, I beg their pardon, they must have changed their name: the German Sudeten Party, it sounds more peaceful! Yes, so Konrad Henlein, the Sudeten Nazi, will call for his region's independence in the name of self-rule for the people, and our dear Adi will immediately mass his troops along the Czechoslovakian border. Now he need only to threaten the world with all-out war and he'll be able to cross the border and his blood brothers will welcome him with open arms and bouquets of flowers like some messiah. That's what he did with Saar, the Rhineland and Austria, he'll do the same with Sudeten, the Carpathians and then all of Czechoslovakia, and it'll be Poland next, and maybe the Netherlands, France, and—who knows—why not the USSR or the United States? Hitler's a pacifist: and the proof is that he's not starting wars, he's protecting German populations. He doesn't invade countries, he annexes them. Unarmed, because they're handed to him on a plate. No point fighting, he just has to open his mouth for people to comply with his whims. He's like a spoiled child who gets his own way by rolling on the floor screaming. So it's bad luck for anyone over there who's not a "pureblood" by birth…the Communists, the democrats, homosexuals, the sick, Romanies and, of course, Jews—it's prison for all of them! The purification started in Vienna, and it's going on all the time in Munich, and in Dachau concentration camp."

"But Dachau can't hold the whole population of Europe!" Mama points out. "That's enough of that, you're talking nonsense. And you'll frighten Bürschi."

"I'm just joking, my love. You're not frightened, are you, my little Bürschi?"

I bury my face against him and he puts his arms around me. I think of Aunt Bella, who thought she was escaping danger by moving to Prague. In Berlin she proudly showed me her passport and encouraged me to convince my parents we should join her.

"We were right not to immigrate there," says my father, as if reading my thoughts. "We're safer right under his nose. His genius is so far-reaching he's forgotten to look out of his own window. If he only knew!"

Everything happens as my father has predicted. Konrad Henlein's paramilitary forces relentlessly victimize the so-called non-Aryan population in the Sudetens and clash with the regular army. Hitler announces that German troops will cross the frontier to establish some order, his mind is made up about that. France and England, both allies of Czechoslovakia, ought to announce war on us if the Wehrmacht ever sets foot on Czechoslovakian soil. Instead, France's Édouard Daladier and England's Neville Chamberlain come to Munich to listen to the Nazi arguments, hoping for an honorable compromise, or at least an acceptable one. The American president, Roosevelt, calls for peace.

1938

"Anything but war, that's all they can think of," my father explains to my mother. "But Hitler wants war. And he'll have it one way or another. It's there in black and white in his book."

Chamberlain tests the water with a quick preliminary visit and is received at the Eagle's Nest in Berchtesgaden, just a few hours from here, up in the mountains that we see from the lakes in summer. After a walk through the Alpine scenery and a vegetarian lunch, the British dignitary came away having secured nothing but unpleasant remarks: Hitler was in a sullen mood, the diplomats reported.

"He must have treated him like a little pen-pusher," my father translates, and laughs as he adds, "or maybe even like a Jew. Who knows?"

Once back in London, and having consulted his French counterpart, Neville Chamberlain agreed to return to Germany for further negotiations. The two men are here now, on the corner of our street.

"Benito Mussolini was invited to join the masquerade as well," Papa muses, "as if he was one of the negotiators."


Our apartment is like an antechamber for the conference. Newspapers are spread open over my father's desk. There are pictures of Adolf Hitler in his double-breasted jacket and Nazi armband, Benito Mussolini in military uniform, Neville Chamberlain dressed like a city banker, and Édouard Daladier in a pin-striped gray suit, the four of them gathered at the Führerbau in Munich. Also present are Hermann Göring, an imposing figure in white ceremonial dress, his marshal's baton in his hand, and Count Ciano, freshly appointed as the youngest foreign affairs minister by his father-in-law, Il Duce. That was the day before yesterday, Thursday, September 29. They signed a peace treaty that night.

"Remember that date," Papa tells me, "like January 30, 1933, when our neighbor became chancellor. Remember September 30, 1938, Bürschi, remember it all your life, the day France and England abandoned Czechoslovakia to the Nazis."

Shortly after midday the next day, Hitler invited Neville Chamberlain to tea at his home. The vast procession of cars dispersed in a blast of engine sound, like a great flock of black eagles taking flight. For me it was just a day like any other, a dazzlingly sunny Friday afternoon in the fall. I was walking along the opposite sidewalk on my way home from school while our Führer treated the aging English statesman to a visit of our street. Next they stopped at the Brasserie Bürgerbräu, where Hitler gave his first speeches, then in front of the Feldherrnhalle, where his attempted coup was quashed in 1923. Hitler acknowledged the monument with a brief gesture like a priest making the sign of the cross before a crucifix. Mussolini had already returned to Italy in the night and Daladier, who had declined the invitation, was flying back to Paris. And our life simply picked up where it had left off.

■ ■ ■

After the conference of September 29, 1938, while Chamberlain and Daladier were being "welcomed home as heroes," our Reich swallowed up the Sudetenland and grew overnight by thirty thousand square kilometers and three million inhabitants. This period of peace, the "Peace of the Third Reich," would last a thousand years, according to Hitler. At noon our troops took possession of these new territories. On September 30 Poland took control of the Czechoslovakian town of Teschen and of the Zaolzie region. On November 1, Poland invaded the northern territories of Spisz and Orava. On November 2, Hungary annexed further Slovak territories, Upper Hungary and sub-Carpathian Ruthenia. In three months Czechoslovakia lost forty thousand square kilometers and five million inhabitants.

Here in Munich signs have appeared on the doors of public premises saying: "No Jews." Jewish shops are identified with a Star of David painted in red, and then their windows are smashed.

On November 7, a young man attacked the Nazi diplomat Ernst vom Rath, in Paris. The assassin was a German Jew called Herschel Grynszpan. In a letter to his uncle he claimed he had "committed this act so the whole world would hear him."

Today, November 9, there's much pomp in Munich surrounding celebrations to mark the aborted putsch of 1923: the SS are parading through the streets all over the city. But Ernst vom Rath has just died, despite intervention from Hitler's personal physician. His death is announced on the radio, and the sounds of shouting, explosions and breaking glass reach us from the street. The sky glows orange through the night.

My mother is silent. Papa is ashen. The telephone never stops ringing. In a tentative shaky voice, Papa tells my mother what various callers have told him:

The Herzog-Rudolf Synagogue is in flames. Jewish shops marked out with the Star of David are being looted. And this is happening all over Germany: in Marburg, Tübingen, Cologne, Leipzig, Esslingen, Treuchtlingen…In Vienna in Austria, they're burning synagogues, desecrating cemeteries and killing Jews. They're beating women, children and the elderly. We must leave.

"But how can we, Luidgie, my darling, how can we? Look outside, they've gone mad. And where would we go?"

"We'll see about that tomorrow. Let's turn out the lights, draw the curtains, lock the doors and go to bed. We'll leave tomorrow."

■ ■ ■

Alone in my room, I can't get to sleep. I lie in my bed listening to shouting in the street and watching my bedroom curtains flushed orange by the blazing sky. I fall asleep at last and have a nightmare: someone's knocking at our door. No, I'm not dreaming, it really is our door that they're hammering. It's here. They're here. The Gestapo are at our apartment. They've come for my family. They've come in. They're in the drawing room. It's still dark outside. I can hear them. Their voices are curt. I hear my father's voice. And my mother's. Mama and Papa are frightened. I hear men shouting. Yelling at my parents. They open the door to my bedroom. Soldiers. In uniform.

They turn on the lights. My mother's in the drawing room. Where's Papa? He comes out of his bedroom. He's dressed now, flanked by two men. He comes over to me, takes my head in his hands, kisses me. They take him away. They're arresting him. They're arresting my father.

"Don't worry, Bürschi!"

He told me not to worry.

They're going to kill him. No, I mustn't worry. There's no point. It won't change anything. They won't kill him. He's gone now. We're alone. His voice has gone, the noise has ended. I want to see him. I want him to be here. I don't want him to die. I don't want to die. Why us? I want to open my eyes, to wake up. But, sadly, this isn't a dream. It's real life. They've arrested Papa. They've put my father in prison. They've taken him away.


The next day, they came back to take the books from his bookshelves. My mother asked whether they would be putting the books in a safe place *too*.

"What else is there for you to take from us now?" she added.

They looked at us, and I regretted what Mama had said. They didn't even close the door when they left.


Two days already. I've stopped going to school. They've arrested Uncle Fritz, Papa's brother. His wife, Aunt Erna, who has the same first name as Mama, is with us now. Mama's comforting her.

"More than twenty thousand Jews," she sobs, "more than twenty thousand arrested in Germany and Austria. What are they going to do to them?"

The days drag by in silence.

Five days. No news.

November 16. Nothing. Aunt Erna and my mother have decided to make preparations to flee. There are rumors that Jews' assets are to be confiscated. A dealer comes to inventory the valuable objects in our apartment. The next day the same old man comes back with two removal men to take everything my mother hands over to him. He points out ornaments and items of furniture to the packers with a withering tilt of his chin. They take our paintings and silver. The old man leaves wads of bills for my mother.

"They're just trinkets," he says. "Count yourself lucky. If you knew the things I took from the Bernheimers, a whole different story! And I didn't pay them much more than I have you!"

A week has gone by. We have no news of my father. We've received new identity cards by mail. They're special papers for Jews. Every Jewish man now has to add the Hebrew first name "Israel" to his name, and for women it's "Sarah." My name's now Edgar-Israel, my father is Ludwig-Israel, and my mother is Erna-Sarah.

Fritz and Papa are imprisoned in Dachau camp. Mama discovered that today, and went there with Aunt Erna. Over the gates to the camp are the words "*Arbeit*

1938

*macht frei*," "work sets you free." They weren't allowed in but they left a parcel of provisions for Fritz and Papa.

It's now ten days. Mama cries a lot and I'm not allowed out of the house. Aunt Bobbie does our shopping for us. The curtains are drawn the whole time so we live in darkness. Outside it's snowing. I pull the curtain aside slightly and watch the snowflakes swirl in the street. In the evenings the lights are on in Hitler's apartment.

I played piano this afternoon.

Two weeks. Fourteen days and fourteen nights. Nothing.

December 1. Twenty days. I play piano with the mute pedal on so as not to make too much noise. I'm alone in the apartment, and I mustn't open the door to anyone. Mama's gone out, she's gone to ask for help from a former author of my father's, Dr. Wilhelm Grau, a member of the Reich Institute for the History of the New Germany, who runs the research department for the "Jewish question." In 1934 he published a study on the Jewish community in Regensburg. It's dark now. She's still not home.

The door opens at last.

Her eyes are red.

"He said there's nothing he can do."

Aunt Erna came over again today. There are more than eleven thousand prisoners in Dachau.

It will be Christmas soon and we've had no news of my father for four weeks.

I stayed home alone again all day today. Mama came home exhausted. She spent the day visiting all sorts of administrative offices but didn't achieve anything.

We learn a little more every day about this camp, which since 1933 has been run by Munich's chief of police, Heinrich Himmler, an SS officer close to Adolf Hitler. Dachau was set up in a former munitions factory. The first prisoners had to do the construction work themselves, using their bare hands to build their own bunkhouses and those for the SS guarding them. The Nazis have published photographs depicting the camp as an exemplary place for "re-education," complete with a swimming pool—some prisoners would be happier there than in their own homes! The truth is, it's a place where they execute prisoners. Aunt Erna told us that Hans Beimler, a member of the KPD, the German Communist Party, who was interned in 1933, managed to escape and published a book in Great Britain and the USSR, chronicling everyday life in these camps.

1938

"But why don't the Russians, French, English and Americans say anything?" Mama asks. "I just can't understand how Daladier and Chamberlain could sit drinking tea with Hitler when they knew about this. Why don't they intervene?"

I don't think Papa will ever come home.

It's been over a month.

■ ■ ■

December 20. He's home! But I hardly recognized him. A shriveled little man with a shaven head and thin body, his eyes sunken in dark sockets, his gray face patched with purplish-blue bruises. He stood hunched on the doorstep, swimming in his clothes that were now too big for him. He took me in his arms and I was wracked with sobs. He didn't speak. I think he wanted to, but the sounds wouldn't come out of his mouth, his body shook as much as mine. Mama appeared. She gave a little cry and clung to the two of us. Night was falling. We stood motionless in the doorway, huddled together. Papa didn't want to tell us anything about it. He went off to bed.

The next day he still lay there. Mama took him his meals in bed. Over the next few days, he started getting up, and soon he was back as the elegant, shaved, fragranced man he had been, taking breakfast in his same suit from the old days, a little roomier than it had been, leafing through the morning papers, taking notes again, and occasionally scowling furiously toward the window, before going back to his usual place at his desk, drafting letters in his clear, precise handwriting, and sending me out to post them for him as he used to.

"We're going to leave, Bürschi," he tells me one evening by the light of our menorah, which is lit for once. "You'll see, we're going to leave this hell behind, and we'll finally stop living opposite that man, that bastard."

I've never heard him curse. It's Christmas Eve. On the other side of the street, Adolf Hitler spends the festive evening alone, as usual, served by Frau Winter.

1938

*By defending myself against the Jew, I am fighting for the work of the Lord.*

—ADOLF HITLER, *MEIN KAMPF*

I'll be fifteen soon and Hitler's been living opposite us for ten years now. Mama tells me that when I was little he was less famous than Uncle Lion. He even helped my uncle on with his coat once, treating him to a "Herr Feuchtwanger" on the terrace of Café Heck, where my father used to order lemonade.

In the public gardens where Jews are now banned, I used to play with my hoop and chase pigeons. I like it when Mama reminds me of my childhood in the days of the Weimar Republic, before the Nazis, before Adolf Hitler became chancellor. Germany was a democracy, we were free. At the time of the great crash, when Munich was so poor and you were in danger of being robbed on every street corner, beggars used to greet us in the street because they knew my uncle's books. They came to the house and we'd let them share in my favorite meal: hot crispy sausages. My father was an editor. I'd set off in the mornings with Rosie, a young woman who lived at home with us and loved me like a mother. Memories come flooding back...Rosie must have left when the racial laws were introduced. My mother often played tennis on the courts behind our house. My father sometimes worked in the drawing room. Writers would come visit him, and I used to serve them tea. In summer he would send me out to deliver books to his writer friends. I went to Thomas Mann's house with Rosie, and made it a point of honor to be the one who carried those precious parceled-up-with-string books that the two men exchanged. We used to go away for weekends to glorious lakes where we rented villas; we spent the summer staying with friends' families. Yes, I remember my childhood...I was often invited to birthday teas with Aryan friends. We didn't say "Aryan" in those days. We didn't say anything. There was no distinction.

We don't go out now so my mother tells me stories all day long. She describes her younger days and my childhood. It was fun, she says. When she talks about those years, her smile lights up her face again, and I could listen to her for hours. I forget the drawn curtains, the gray skies and the SS pacing the sidewalks. She and my father used to go to parties that went on all night, and they'd totter home smiling happily. It was the Roaring Twenties. They were good years, she says.

"Bavaria's a magnificent country, my darling, with its onion-shaped church towers and its green, flower-filled meadows. It will be like that again one day."

■ ■ ■

Application forms for visas are piling up on the table in the drawing room. We fill out new ones every day and open the letters of reply in the mornings. They're always negative. Today's form is for El Salvador. I study in detail the entry about this country in the encyclopedia, and picture myself exploring this land with its twenty volcanoes. The main thing is the ocean, and beaches over twelve miles long. I've never seen the sea. At night I pray we'll be able to escape. I beg the Lord not to call me to him before I've seen the horizon.

When my father tells us we've been granted a family visa for Great Britain I don't whoop for joy. My first thought is to wonder how I'll live there when I don't speak the language. I've lost the habit of celebrating anything, and I daren't now. And yet I feel something not unlike happiness. We can leave. Uncle Heinrich fought valiantly from Paris to secure this visa. He contacted my father's sisters in Palestine and Uncle Lion in the South of France, as well as my uncle by marriage Jacob Reich. Between them they amassed the thousand pounds needed to buy the visa. Thanks to a contribution from a London-based organization and through its connections in the Jewish community in Bavaria, our file managed to be submitted to the British Foreign Office, and now it's received official confirmation.

1939

I'll leave first, on February 14, 1939, in ten days' time, and my parents will join me in a few weeks. I'll make the journey alone, taking the train across Germany and the Netherlands, and a boat over the English Channel, then by rail again up to London. A friend of a former colleague of my father's will be waiting for me at the station and will accompany me across London to catch another train. A volunteer English family will host me until my parents arrive. No one knows how long that will be. Before they come, they need to arrange for our belongings to be shipped, and will probably have to abandon the most valuable. By Nazi law, these things belong to the German people and not to the grasping hooked fingers of the Jews we are.

Since we received confirmation that we're leaving for London, I can't help smiling when I see the Führer's window lit up at night. He doesn't know I'm watching him, or that I'm here at all; he has no inkling that here, just opposite his apartment, a child has grown up over the last ten years, a child who will one day bear witness. My heart beats harder when I walk past the window. I still jump at the sound of an engine starting up in the night or footsteps on the stairs in the early hours.

I look at the furniture in our apartment, the door handles that I'll never hold in my hand again, the molding on the ceiling, the shadows on the floor when the sun spills through the house. If I survive, if I leave, I'll be happy, I swear it.

My parents are in the drawing room making a list of things we have to leave behind. We're not allowed to take traditional objects that are now the property of the "German nation." On that basis, the menorah that belonged to my great-grandparents has to stay.

"But that's absurd," says my father, "you can't get more Jewish than a menorah! We've only ever used it once, this Christmas, and actually I wonder why now!"

My mother can't find any way to calm him. He's shouting. I've never seen him like this.

"It doesn't matter, my darling. You yourself have said it's pointless, it's no more than a knickknack."

"But it belonged to my ancestors. I've known it all my life, it's ours. What are they going to do with it?"

"Melt it down probably…"

Papa blanches at the thought, picks up the candelabra, throws it to the floor and tramples on it, screaming, "Well, let them melt it down, let them!"

Mama stays silent. The menorah's reduced to a hunk of gnarled metal. Mama goes over to him, puts her arm around him, holds him to her and kisses his neck.

My father and I are walking through the main station in Munich. He's carrying my suitcase. He's loaned me one of his suits. I can feel the chill wind sneaking through the weft of my scarf, and I puff out my chest. Soldiers check our papers. I have a one-way ticket to London, a passport, and a visa that's perfectly in order. Papa has a return ticket to Emmerich on the Dutch border. They let us through without a flicker. In my head I practice the English sentences I've been learning frantically in the

last few days: "My name is Edgar"; "How do you do?";
"How old are you?"; and the one that I know I'll never
have to utter: "I am a Jew."

Bavarian landscapes, that I hope not to see again,
unfurl through the window. Cows watch the train
pass, along with farmworkers who I can't help feeling
look bovine too. They're working in the fields, leaning
in toward plows drawn by oxen, wearing traditional
costumes that—I don't know why—remind me of the
Führer. My father doesn't speak. He looks outside, holding my hand in his; his face, which I can see reflected in
the window, suddenly looks calm; I almost think there's
a whiff of hope playing in the corner of his lips. Our eyes
meet. Mine fill with tears. I bury my face against him.

Here we are at the border. I go to the door of the carriage
with him. An SS soldier checks his papers. He asks Papa
curtly why he too isn't leaving Germany, indicating me
with a disdainful nod. My father doesn't reply. And neither do I. I know that deep inside him, and for the first
time, he's not afraid. We have nothing to fear today. In a
few days we won't be German anymore. Ever more.

Papa alighted from the train. I went back to my compartment. On the platform he walked alongside the train as it
slowly pulled away. He pressed his hand to the window,
I put mine against his, we smiled at each other. The train
left. And he disappeared, swallowed up in the darkness.

# DECEMBER
## 2016

*A state which in this age of racial poisoning dedicates itself to the care of its best racial elements must some day become lord of the earth.*

*May the adherents of our movement never forget this if ever the magnitude of the sacrifices should beguile them to an anxious comparison with the possible results.*

— ADOLF HITLER, LAST LINES OF *MEIN KAMPF*

From that last journey, I remember only smells.

The noise of the train has been buried in my memory, as have the faces of other passengers, their voices and the content of their conversations.

I've forgotten what I thought about as I left the land of my childhood, leaving behind my parents and all my memories.

All I remember is the smell of sea spray when the train drew into the Hook of Holland.

I'm now ninety-two years old and I can smell it still.

It was nighttime.

I heard the murmur of waves mingling with the sound of the wind.

We boarded a liner. In the dark of night it was still impossible to make out the sea that I so desperately wanted to see. It finally appeared at dawn.

And, for the first time, I saw the horizon.

# EPILOGUE

For revisionists who might question the veracity of this account—taking, as they do, perverse pleasure in doubting anything from the period—we'd like to clarify that only small details, such as what the weather was like on a specific winter day while scrumptious sausages were sizzling in the kitchen, could conceivably be contestable. It is true that Edgar doesn't clearly remember the exact menu every day, or the temperature outside, or even the pattern of the tie his father chose on a particular morning. Those memories had to be augmented with additional detail. A bit. A tiny bit. Hardly at all. Because Edgar's memory is teeming with such sensory memories from his childhood in Germany. Edgar's life, in the ten years he lived opposite the most abominable individual the world has brought forth, is a ravel of poetic images and monstrous events.

Edgar was born in 1924. Hitler moved in across the road in 1929. Edgar often encountered him on the street. Sometimes he's not sure whether the memories are really his own or his mother's, because she described them to him so often. This is true of his earliest memories. Then everything becomes very clear. And, like everyone else, he can distinguish between what he saw himself and what he was told or what was in the papers at the time or in the history books he's subsequently studied.

In 1929, when Edgar was five, Hitler was forty. Four years younger than Edgar's father, Ludwig. This was four years before Hitler became chancellor, but he was already a major topic of conversation for the family, and everyone in the neighborhood knew he'd just moved in. There was a great deal of talk about him. Edgar's uncle Lion Feucht-wanger, then forty-one, had just published *Jud Süß* about the lives of Germany's Jews in the eighteenth century. With this book he became the German author with the highest international sales. He was one of the most famous personalities on Germany's cultural scene. And he was so preoccupied with the rise of his brother's neighbor that he decided to make him the subject of his next manuscript. This new book provoked such fury in Nazi ranks that they stripped Lion of his nationality as soon as they came to power. Abroad at the time, he could then never return to Germany. Adolf Hitler's ascent to power was therefore a key preoccupation of the Feuchtwangers'.

As Edgar grew up, he continued to meet Hitler in the street, and he watched the tyrant's progress: a few more acolytes every day, the processions of cars growing ever longer, and the people who visited him ever more prestigious. Hitler may not have known who this child surreptitiously watching him was, but Edgar certainly knew about him, just as he recognized members of the Nazi general staff who revolved around him. Munich was the party's capital. It was here that Hitler had attempted his first aborted putsch in 1923, an episode that led to a prison sentence (during which he wrote *Mein Kampf*), here too that the party had its headquarters, the Brown House, and the villas of the SA leader, Ernst Röhm, and Hitler's photographer, Heinrich Hoffman, along with Hitler's favorite restaurant, Osteria, and many other places familiar to locals.

Rarely has the expression "in the devil's lair" been so apt: Hitler can be seen as the incarnation of evil. Never in the history of mankind has so much power been concentrated in a single person. Never has the world hung so fully on the thoughts, desires, whims and deranged extravagances of a single man.

The years 1929 to 1939 may well have seen the greatest concentration of events in modern history. Not one week went by without Hitler's unilaterally deciding to introduce a procedure, institute a law or—later—launch an invasion. And with each of these actions, Edgar had to adapt to a new life because, although he didn't realize it until the Nazi Party forced him to when they came to power in 1933, Edgar came from a family of Jewish faith. Before 1935 Ludwig and Erna Feuchtwanger were not practicing Jews. They almost never went to the synagogue. They were what is known as nonobservant. In their own minds they were Germans and, first and foremost, human beings. That was how they'd intended to raise Edgar. And yet Edgar had no choice but to see himself as threatened, in danger. As of May 1, 1933, three months after Hitler came to power, Edgar's schoolmistress had him draw swastikas in his exercise book. He was eight years old.

This firsthand account, then, charts Edgar's growing awareness not of his own identity but of the identity that other people decided to give him; or rather, one other person, the man who happened to be his neighbor, Adolf Hitler.

When Edgar left Germany, eight months before the Second World War broke out, he was fifteen. He'd been living opposite Hitler for ten years. Three thousand six hundred days and nights. Three thousand six hundred times he could go to bed wondering whether Hitler was going to bed too, and three thousand six hundred times he could wonder over breakfast whether Hitler was already up and what new insanity he would introduce that day. As Edgar reached adolescence he was haunted by these thoughts: Is he there? What's he doing? Does he want to kill us? Will he kill us? Why? Why us? Why me?

I met Edgar in 1995. It is now 2016 so it's been twenty-one years. The British daily newspaper *The Independent* had published a brief article about a Jewish child who'd lived opposite Hitler in Munich from 1929 to 1939: Edgar Feuchtwanger. I was a reporter for the French magazine *VSD*. I called the senior editor of *The Independent*, who gave me a telephone number for the author of the piece, Edgar's daughter Antonia. She was happy to pass on her father's number to me. Only minutes later a meeting had been set up, and the following weekend I was at his house.

I came with a photographer, Nicolas Reynard. We spent the day chatting over cups of tea served by Edgar's charming wife, Primrose. Edgar described life in Munich under Hitler's rule. The life of Jews under the Third Reich. His family's life. He described the Führer's facial expressions, those he himself had seen. With a child's eye, because he often passed him in the street as a boy. He remembers major figures such as Ernst Röhm, Neville Chamberlain, Benito Mussolini and several others who walked past under his window over a ten-year period. He showed us his school exercise book with pencil drawings of swastikas. Nicolas took a black and white photograph of Edgar at his window. And we left.

Since then I've often encouraged Edgar to write his memoirs. But he's a historian: to his academic mind, the life of anonymous individuals isn't necessarily worth telling. And he had so many other books to write! So time went by and still he didn't want to tell his story. We kept in touch, calling, writing—letters at first, then emails. Sometimes chatting on Skype.

The first time we met, Edgar was seventy and I twenty-five. He is now ninety-two and I'm forty-seven. Nicolas Reynard died in a plane crash on an expedition. Primrose passed away in 2012. "I'm starting to think about eternity," Edgar told me. The time had come to write this book. And so at last we set off on the trail of his childhood in Munich. Before it all faded. Was lost. Just in time.

*Bertil Scali*
*December 2016*

# WHAT BECAME OF THEM?

Erna and Ludwig Feuchtwanger, Edgar's parents, were able to leave Germany a few weeks after he did, in May 1939, only months before Nazi troops invaded Poland on September 1. They managed to secure the necessary authorizations to immigrate to England. After a brief stopover in London, they joined their son in Winchester and set up home there, re-creating something of the world they had lost in this new country whose language they didn't even speak. Sadly, only eighteen months after his release from Dachau camp, Ludwig was interned again, this time on the Isle of Man. He was not imprisoned for being a Jew, but mistrusted because he was German. After what was effectively a comfortable stay in comparison with the conditions of his German detention—which he survived only miraculously—he was freed and rejoined his family. After a whole second life during which he worked successively as a private German tutor, a consultant for the US Army and then a researcher into the Third Reich's correspondence, he died in 1947 at the age of sixty-one. Erna lived happily in the community around Winchester until 1979. She continued preparing delicious German meals in her ancient stewpot, something of a Munich Prometheus that she wouldn't have surrendered to the Nazis for anything in the world. This cast-iron receptacle still simmers away on Edgar's stove from time to time. The smells that hover around it in winter make clear references to its owner's tastes—which have remained resolutely Bavarian.

Lion Feuchtwanger was imprisoned in the Camp des Milles near Aix-en-Provence by the French police, who were soon to hand him over to the Nazis. He managed to extricate himself thanks to the intervention of the US consul in Marseille, on the insistence of Eleanor Roosevelt. He immigrated to the United States, where he pursued his writing career in Pacific Palisades, which became an intellectual hub for German émigrés. His friends, including Bertolt Brecht, Thomas and Heinrich Mann and Franz Werfel, regularly convened there. He died in 1958. His wife, Marta, who lived until 1987, kept up a substantial correspondence with Edgar's mother, and later with Edgar himself.

Fritz Feuchtwanger was also released from Dachau on Christmas Eve 1938. He and his wife, Erna, were able to take exile in the United States at the very last minute. Franziska Diamant and her husband managed to flee there just before the war. Uncle Berthold, who did everything differently, succeeded in embarking for Peru just in time. Dorle, Edgar's half sister, lived all her life in Switzerland. For the purposes of this account, some aspects of her private life have been modified. Dorle's mother, Aunt Lilly, also survived the war, first in Berlin and then in a village in Bavaria.

Bella Feuchtwanger, Edgar's aunt who was so happy she could move freely around Germany under the Third Reich thanks to her Czechoslovakian passport, and could continue working for her brother Martin Feuchtwanger's news agency, was arrested by the Nazis when they invaded Prague. She perished in Theresienstadt.

Edgar's childhood friend Beate Siegel, the daughter of one of the first Jews to be publicly beaten and exhibited in the streets of Munich in 1933 with a sign around his neck saying "I'm a Jew and I'll never criticize the police again," left Germany thanks to the British Kindertransport program. Her parents and her brother, Peter Siegel, left for Lima in Peru in 1940, and Peter became a rabbi there. Beate now lives in London, and occasionally in the South of France, near Toulouse, where she read the page proofs of the French original of this book on her computer.

Bobbie Heckelmann, "Aunt Bobbie," and Duke Luitpold of Bavaria, who were not Jews, stayed in Germany and survived the bombing. Edgar and his mother met up with Aunt Bobbie in 1957 and went to the opera with her in Salzburg. Edgar remembers that, ever the socialite, Aunt Bobbie had invited a Saxe-Coburg-Gotha princess for the occasion. Her sister Friedl, who'd married the Hanoverian industrialist Hermann Wolff, also survived. Edgar visited the couple in 1966. Hermann, whose company had used Jews imprisoned in concentration camps as its workforce during the war, was tried after the Liberation. Speaking to Edgar, Hermann Wolff praised Adolf Hitler's extraordinary energy, as if struggling to justify something. His embarrassing monologue petered out into a still more embarrassing stony silence. Friedl's daughter, Arabella, had moved to New York.

Edgar never knew what became of Rosie, one of the young women who rocked him in her arms, brought him up and walked him to the park, and then later to school all through his childhood, and who had to leave the family when the employment of "Aryans" by "Jews" was banned. Her character, a composite of several young Bavarian country girls, has been filled out in this book in order to give the reader a broader understanding of the political and social context of the time. Edgar has no better information about the fate of the building's caretaker, the perennially well-informed Funk. Similarly, Edgar knows nothing about the life of young Ralph, the school friend who invited him to his birthday parties up until the first anti-Semitic laws came into play in 1933, before more than 90 percent of Germans voted to give total power to the Führer.

Mr. and Mrs. Ernst Bernheimer and their daughter, Ingrid, immigrated to Cuba in 1941, it being the only country that would agree to take them. They could have left Germany much earlier, and for a more obvious country such as the United States. But Ingrid's mother had a brother with Down syndrome, and no country was happy to take him. Karli was due to be "euthanized" by the Nazis, but the family's immigration to Cuba saved him in extremis. Other members of the family, Otto Bernheimer and his family, survived by striking a deal with Hermann Göring—selling him paintings by great masters in exchange for a crust of bread, buying a ranch in Venezuela for the marshal's aunt who was married to a Jew...but that's a whole other story!

Eight months after Edgar left Germany, Adolf Hitler ordered his troops to invade Poland. Up in his apartment, he must have gloated presidentially about this latest pacific conquest. This time, though, France and Great Britain honored their commitments and their principles and declared war on Germany. Thanks to an interplay of international alliances, this escalated into a global conflict that cost the lives of fifty million people. All through the war, German Nazis—with the help of the sympathizers in Austria, Czechoslovakia, Poland, the Ukraine, Italy, Greece, France and every other country they crossed—pursued their anti-Semitic policies that annihilated more than six million Jews, Romanies, homosexuals and other minorities. The Allies eventually triumphed over Hitler, who committed suicide in a bunker in Berlin. A little while later, the American photographer Lee Miller posed naked in the Führer's bathtub, just opposite where Edgar had lived, for an article put together with David E. Sherman for *Vogue* magazine.

Hitler's Munich apartment was turned into a police station after the war. There is nothing now to show that the Führer once lived there.

Edgar still lives in the village of Dean near Winchester, in the county of Hampshire, as he has since a few months after he arrived in Great Britain on February 15, 1939. He was taken in by a volunteer family in Cornwall, the wonderful Malcolm and Beryl Dyson—in their early thirties, the parents of a five-year-old and a three-year-old—who taught him to speak English in a matter of months. In September 1939 he obtained a study grant for the prestigious Winchester College. After the war he studied history at the University of Cambridge, then went on to teach and write about history, specializing in subjects such as the reign of Queen Victoria, the history of Prussia and the careers of Britain's prime ministers Disraeli and Gladstone, as well—of course—as the history of twentieth-century Germany. In 1962 he married a young Englishwoman, Primrose, whose father had been one of the generals in the 1944 Normandy campaign. Edgar is now ninety-two. He has three children and now has three grandchildren. The German state awarded him the Federal Cross of Merit for his services to Anglo-German relations. He would like to be remembered as an "honorary Englishman."

This book was written in Munich, Paris, Winchester and London, based on Edgar's recollections, his family memoirs published in Germany by the publishing company where his father used to work, Duncker & Humblot (*Erlebnis und Geschichte: Als Kind in Hitlers Deutschland—Ein Leben in England*),* numerous contemporaneous documents such as issues of *L'Illustration*,

---

*"Experience and History: A Childhood in Hitler's Germany—A Life in England."

*Paris-Match* and *Paris-Soir*, audiovisual documents such as newsreels from Germany, France, Great Britain and the United States, and the books of Lion Feuchtwanger, particularly *Jud Süß* and *Success*, as well as the work of his then rival in bookstores *Mein Kampf*, whose author — a vegetarian — didn't like Bavarian sausages with their chargrilled flavor, although they are famously delicious.

EDGAR FEUCHTWANGER was born in Munich in 1924 and immigrated to England in 1939. He studied at Cambridge University and taught history at the University of Southampton until he retired in 1989. His major works include *From Weimar to Hitler*, *Disraeli*, and *Imperial Germany 1850–1918*. In 2003 he received the Order of Merit of the Federal Republic of Germany for promoting Anglo-German relations.

BERTIL SCALI is a French journalist and writer. He wrote and co-directed a TV documentary about Edgar Feuchtwanger's childhood in Munich, and is the author of *Villa Windsor*.

ADRIANA HUNTER studied French and Drama at the University of London. She has translated more than fifty books including Camille Laurens's *Who You Think I Am* and Hervé Le Tellier's *Eléctrico W*, winner of the French-American Foundation's 2013 Translation Prize in Fiction. She won the 2011 Scott Moncrieff Prize, and her work has been short-listed twice for the Independent Foreign Fiction Prize. She lives in Kent, England.

# ▣ OTHER PRESS

*You might also enjoy these titles from our list:*

### WHEN MEMORY COMES by Saul Friedländer

A classic of Holocaust literature, the eloquent, acclaimed memoir of childhood, now reissued with an introduction by Claire Messud

"Friedländer undertakes an evocative journey into his past that is likely to leave many a reader shaken."
—Amos Elon, *New York Times Book Review*

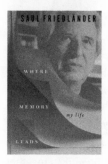

### WHERE MEMORY LEADS by Saul Friedländer

A Pulitzer Prize–winning historian's return to memoir, a tale of intellectual coming-of-age on three continents

"A gripping, troubling narrative... Page after page we feel we are getting closer to [Friedländer]. Then we suddenly realize how inscrutable an individual life is — to us, to the narrator himself." —Carlo Ginzburg

### NOT I: MEMOIRS OF A GERMAN CHILDHOOD by Joachim Fest

A searing portrait of an intellectually rigorous German household opposed to the Nazis and how its members suffered for their political stance

"Quietly compelling, elegantly expressed... *Not I* shrinks the Wagnerian scale of German history in the 1930s and 1940s to chamber music dimensions. It is intensely personal, clear-eyed, and absolutely riveting." —*New York Times*

*Also recommended:*

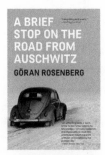

## A BRIEF STOP ON THE ROAD FROM AUSCHWITZ by Göran Rosenberg
WINNER OF THE AUGUST PRIZE

A shattering memoir about a father's attempt to survive the aftermath of Auschwitz

"A towering and wondrous work about memory and experience, exquisitely crafted, humane, generous, devastating, yet somehow also hopeful." —*Financial Times*

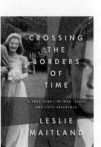

## CROSSING THE BORDERS OF TIME by Leslie Maitland

A dramatic true story of World War II, exile, and love lost — then reclaimed

"*Schindler's List* meets *Casablanca* in this tale of a daughter's epic search for her mother's prewar beau — fifty years later." —*Good Housekeeping*

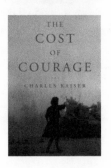

## THE COST OF COURAGE by Charles Kaiser

The heroic true story of the three youngest children of a bourgeois Catholic family who worked together in the French Resistance

"A thorough and quite accessible history of Europe's six-year murderous paroxysm... *The Cost of Courage* documents, through the life of an extraordinary family, one of the twentieth century's most fascinating events — the German occupation of the City of Light." —*Wall Street Journal*